SELECTED POETRY

OF

WORLD WAR ONE

Selected Poetry of World War One
By Wilfrid Owen, Siegfried Sassoon, Ivor Gurney, Isaac Rosenberg, Vera
Brittain, Rupert Brooke, Alan Seeger, Robert Graves, Charles Sorley,
Edgell Rickword, and others.

Print ISBN 13: 978-1-4209-8180-3
eBook ISBN 13: 978-1-4209-8181-0

Cover Image: a detail of "Dog Tired", by Christopher Richard Wynne Nevinson,
c. 1916 (oil on canvas) / © Bristol Museums, Galleries & Archives / Purchased,
1954. / Bridgeman Images.

Please visit *www.digireads.com*

CONTENTS

The Poems of Wilfrid Owen

The War Poems of Siegfried Sassoon

THE POEMS OF IVOR GURNEY

SEVERN AND SOMME

WAR'S EMBERS AND OTHER VERSES

POEMS FROM CAMP AND TRENCH BY ISAAC ROSENBERG

VERSES OF A V.A.D

THE WAR SONNETS OF RUPERT BROOKE

SELECTED POEMS OF ALAN SEEGER

SELECTED POEMS OF ROBERT GRAVES

SELECTED POEMS OF CHARLES SORLEY

SELECTED POEMS OF EDGELL RICKWORD

SELECTED POEMS BY VARIOUS AUTHORS

THE POEMS OF WILFRID OWEN

Introduction

In writing an introduction such as this it is good to be brief. The poems printed in this book need no preliminary commendations from me or anyone else. The author has left us his own fragmentary but impressive Foreword; this, and his Poems, can speak for him, backed by the authority of his experience as an infantry soldier, and sustained by nobility and originality of style. All that was strongest in Wilfred Owen survives in his poems; any superficial impressions of his personality, any records of his conversation, behaviour, or appearance, would be irrelevant and unseemly. The curiosity which demands such morsels would be incapable of appreciating the richness of his work.

The discussion of his experiments in assonance and dissonance (of which *Strange Meeting* is the finest example) may be left to the professional critics of verse, the majority of whom will be more preoccupied with such technical details than with the profound humanity of the self-revelation manifested in such magnificent lines as those at the end of his *Apologia pro Poemate Meo*, and in that other poem which he named *Greater Love*.

The importance of his contribution to the literature of the War cannot be decided by those who, like myself, both admired him as a poet and valued him as a friend. His conclusions about War are so entirely in accordance with my own that I cannot attempt to judge his work with any critical detachment. I can only affirm that he was a man of absolute integrity of mind. He never wrote his poems (as so many war-poets did) to make the effect of a personal gesture. He pitied others; he did not pity himself. In the last year of his life he attained a clear vision of what he needed to say, and these poems survive him as his true and splendid testament.

Wilfred Owen was born at Oswestry on 18th March 1893. He was educated at the Birkenhead Institute, and matriculated at London University in 1910. In 1913 he obtained a private tutorship near Bordeaux, where he remained until 1915. During this period he became acquainted with the eminent French poet, Laurent Tailhade, to whom he showed his early verses, and from whom he received considerable encouragement. In 1915, in spite of delicate health, he joined the Artists' Rifles O.T.C., was gazetted to the Manchester Regiment, and served with their 2nd Battalion in France from December 1916 to June 1917, when he was invalided home. Fourteen months later he returned to the Western Front and served with the same Battalion, ultimately commanding a Company.

He was awarded the Military Cross for gallantry while taking part in some heavy lighting on 1st October. He was killed on 4th November 1918, while endeavouring to get his men across the Sambre Canal.

A month before his death he wrote to his mother: "My nerves are in perfect order. I came out again in order to help these boys; directly, by leading them as well as an officer can; indirectly, by watching their sufferings that I may speak of them as well as a pleader can." Let his own words be his epitaph:—

> "Courage was mine, and I had mystery;
> Wisdom was mine, and I had mastery."

SIEGFRIED SASSOON.

Preface

This book is not about heroes. English Poetry is not yet fit to speak of them. Nor is it about deeds or lands, nor anything about glory, honour, dominion or power,

except War.
Above all, this book is not concerned with Poetry.
The subject of it is War, and the pity of War.
The Poetry is in the pity.
Yet these elegies are not to this generation,
This is in no sense consolatory.

They may be to the next.
All the poet can do to-day is to warn.
That is why the true Poets must be truthful.
If I thought the letter of this book would last,
I might have used proper names; but if the spirit of it survives Prussia,—my ambition and those names will be content; for they will have achieved themselves fresher fields than Flanders.

Note.—This Preface was found, in an unfinished condition, among Wilfred Owen's papers.

Strange Meeting

It seemed that out of the battle I escaped
Down some profound dull tunnel, long since scooped
Through granites which titanic wars had groined.
Yet also there encumbered sleepers groaned,
Too fast in thought or death to be bestirred.
Then, as I probed them, one sprang up, and stared
With piteous recognition in fixed eyes,
Lifting distressful hands as if to bless.
And by his smile, I knew that sullen hall;
With a thousand fears that vision's face was grained;
Yet no blood reached there from the upper ground,
And no guns thumped, or down the flues made moan.
"Strange friend," I said, "Here is no cause to mourn."
"None," said the other, "Save the undone years,
The hopelessness. Whatever hope is yours,
Was my life also; I went hunting wild

After the wildest beauty in the world,
Which lies not calm in eyes, or braided hair,
But mocks the steady running of the hour,
And if it grieves, grieves richlier than here.
For by my glee might many men have laughed,
And of my weeping something has been left,
Which must die now. I mean the truth untold,
The pity of war, the pity war distilled.
Now men will go content with what we spoiled.
Or, discontent, boil bloody, and be spilled.
They will be swift with swiftness of the tigress,
None will break ranks, though nations trek from progress.
Courage was mine, and I had mystery;
Wisdom was mine, and I had mastery;
To miss the march of this retreating world
Into vain citadels that are not walled.
Then, when much blood had clogged their chariot-wheels
I would go up and wash them from sweet wells,
Even with truths that lie too deep for taint.
I would have poured my spirit without stint
But not through wounds; not on the cess of war.
Foreheads of men have bled where no wounds were.
I am the enemy you killed, my friend.
I knew you in this dark; for so you frowned
Yesterday through me as you jabbed and killed.
I parried; but my hands were loath and cold.
Let us sleep now . . ."

(This poem was found among the author's papers. It ends on this strange
note.)

Another Version

Earth's wheels run oiled with blood. Forget we that.
Let us lie down and dig ourselves in thought.
Beauty is yours and you have mastery,
Wisdom is mine and I have mystery.
We two will stay behind and keep our troth.
Let us forego men's minds that are brute's natures,
Let us not sup the blood which some say nurtures,
Be we not swift with swiftness of the tigress.
Let us break ranks from those who trek from progress.
Miss we the march of this retreating world
Into old citadels that are not walled.
Let us lie out and hold the open truth.
Then when their blood hath clogged the chariot wheels
We will go up and wash them from deep wells.
What though we sink from men as pitchers falling

Many shall raise us up to be their filling
Even from wells we sunk too deep for war
And filled by brows that bled where no wounds were.

Alternative Line—

Even as One who bled where no wounds were.

Greater Love

Red lips are not so red
    As the stained stones kissed by the English dead.
Kindness of wooed and wooer
Seems shame to their love pure.
O Love, your eyes lose lure
    When I behold eyes blinded in my stead!

Your slender attitude
    Trembles not exquisite like limbs knife-skewed,
Rolling and rolling there
Where God seems not to care;
Till the fierce love they bear
    Cramps them in death's extreme decrepitude.

Your voice sings not so soft,—
    Though even as wind murmuring through raftered loft,—
Your dear voice is not dear,
Gentle, and evening clear,
As theirs whom none now hear,
    Now earth has stopped their piteous mouths that coughed.

Heart, you were never hot
    Nor large, nor full like hearts made great with shot;
And though your hand be pale,
Paler are all which trail
Your cross through flame and hail:
    Weep, you may weep, for you may touch them not.

Apologia Pro Poemate Meo

I, too, saw God through mud,—
    The mud that cracked on cheeks when wretches smiled.
    War brought more glory to their eyes than blood,
    And gave their laughs more glee than shakes a child.

Merry it was to laugh there—
 Where death becomes absurd and life absurder.
 For power was on us as we slashed bones bare
 Not to feel sickness or remorse of murder.

I, too, have dropped off Fear—
 Behind the barrage, dead as my platoon,
 And sailed my spirit surging, light and clear
 Past the entanglement where hopes lay strewn;

And witnessed exultation—
 Faces that used to curse me, scowl for scowl,
 Shine and lift up with passion of oblation,
 Seraphic for an hour; though they were foul.

I have made fellowships—
 Untold of happy lovers in old song.
 For love is not the binding of fair lips
 With the soft silk of eyes that look and long,

By Joy, whose ribbon slips,—
 But wound with war's hard wire whose stakes are strong;
 Bound with the bandage of the arm that drips;
 Knit in the webbing of the rifle-thong.

I have perceived much beauty
 In the hoarse oaths that kept our courage straight;
 Heard music in the silentness of duty;
 Found peace where shell-storms spouted reddest spate.

Nevertheless, except you share
 With them in hell the sorrowful dark of hell,
 Whose world is but the trembling of a flare,
 And heaven but as the highway for a shell,

You shall not hear their mirth:
 You shall not come to think them well content
 By any jest of mine. These men are worth
 Your tears: You are not worth their merriment.

November 1917.

The Show

My soul looked down from a vague height with Death,
As unremembering how I rose or why,
And saw a sad land, weak with sweats of dearth,
Gray, cratered like the moon with hollow woe,
And pitted with great pocks and scabs of plaques.

Across its beard, that horror of harsh wire,
There moved thin caterpillars, slowly uncoiled.
It seemed they pushed themselves to be as plugs
Of ditches, where they writhed and shrivelled, killed.

By them had slimy paths been trailed and scraped
Round myriad warts that might be little hills.

From gloom's last dregs these long-strung creatures crept,
And vanished out of dawn down hidden holes.

(And smell came up from those foul openings
As out of mouths, or deep wounds deepening.)

On dithering feet upgathered, more and more,
Brown strings, towards strings of grey, with bristling spines,
All migrants from green fields, intent on mire.

Those that were gray, of more abundant spawns,
Ramped on the rest and ate them and were eaten.

I saw their bitten backs curve, loop, and straighten.
I watched those agonies curl, lift, and flatten.

Whereat, in terror what the sight might mean,
I reeled and shivered earthward like a feather.

And Death fell with me, like a deepening moan.
And He, picking a manner of worm, which half had hid
Its bruises in the earth, but crawled no further,
Showed me its feet, the feet of many men,
And the fresh-severed head of it, my head.

Mental Cases

Who are these? Why sit they here in twilight?
Wherefore rock they, purgatorial shadows,
Drooping tongues from jaws that slob their relish,
Baring teeth that leer like skulls' tongues wicked?

Stroke on stroke of pain,—but what slow panic,
Gouged these chasms round their fretted sockets?
Ever from their hair and through their hand palms
Misery swelters. Surely we have perished
Sleeping, and walk hell; but who these hellish?

—These are men whose minds the Dead have ravished.
Memory fingers in their hair of murders,
Multitudinous murders they once witnessed.
Wading sloughs of flesh these helpless wander,
Treading blood from lungs that had loved laughter.
Always they must see these things and hear them,
Batter of guns and shatter of flying muscles,
Carnage incomparable and human squander
Rucked too thick for these men's extrication.

Therefore still their eyeballs shrink tormented
Back into their brains, because on their sense
Sunlight seems a bloodsmear; night comes blood-black;
Dawn breaks open like a wound that bleeds afresh.
—Thus their heads wear this hilarious, hideous,
Awful falseness of set-smiling corpses.
—Thus their hands are plucking at each other;
Picking at the rope-knouts of their scourging;
Snatching after us who smote them, brother,
Pawing us who dealt them war and madness.

Parable of the Old Men and the Young

So Abram rose, and clave the wood, and went,
And took the fire with him, and a knife.
And as they sojourned both of them together,
Isaac the first-born spake and said, My Father,
Behold the preparations, fire and iron,
But where the lamb for this burnt-offering?
Then Abram bound the youth with belts and straps,
And builded parapets and trenches there,
And stretchèd forth the knife to slay his son.
When lo! an Angel called him out of heaven,
Saying, Lay not thy hand upon the lad,
Neither do anything to him. Behold,
A ram caught in a thicket by its horns;
Offer the Ram of Pride instead of him.
But the old man would not so, but slew his son. . . .

Arms and the Boy

Let the boy try along this bayonet-blade
How cold steel is, and keen with hunger of blood;
Blue with all malice, like a madman's flash;
And thinly drawn with famishing for flesh.

Lend him to stroke these blind, blunt bullet-leads,
Which long to nuzzle in the hearts of lads,
Or give him cartridges whose fine zinc teeth,
Are sharp with sharpness of grief and death.

For his teeth seem for laughing round an apple.
There lurk no claws behind his fingers supple;
And God will grow no talons at his heels,
Nor antlers through the thickness of his curls.

Anthem for Doomed Youth

What passing-bells for these who die as cattle?
        Only the monstrous anger of the guns.
        Only the stuttering rifles' rapid rattle
Can patter out their hasty orisons.
No mockeries for them; no prayers nor bells,
Nor any voice of mourning save the choirs,—
The shrill, demented choirs of wailing shells;
And bugles calling for them from sad shires.

What candles may be held to speed them all?
        Not in the hands of boys, but in their eyes
Shall shine the holy glimmers of goodbyes.
        The pallor of girls' brows shall be their pall;
Their flowers the tenderness of patient minds,
And each slow dusk a drawing-down of blinds.

The Send-Off

Down the close, darkening lanes they sang their way
To the siding-shed,
And lined the train with faces grimly gay.

Their breasts were stuck all white with wreath and spray
As men's are, dead.

Dull porters watched them, and a casual tramp
Stood staring hard,
Sorry to miss them from the upland camp.
Then, unmoved, signals nodded, and a lamp
Winked to the guard.

So secretly, like wrongs hushed-up, they went.
They were not ours:
We never heard to which front these were sent.

Nor there if they yet mock what women meant
Who gave them flowers.

Shall they return to beatings of great bells
In wild trainloads?
A few, a few, too few for drums and yells,
May creep back, silent, to still village wells,
Up half-known roads.

Insensibility

I

Happy are men who yet before they are killed
Can let their veins run cold.
Whom no compassion fleers
Or makes their feet
Sore on the alleys cobbled with their brothers.
The front line withers,
But they are troops who fade, not flowers
For poets' tearful fooling:
Men, gaps for filling:
Losses, who might have fought
Longer; but no one bothers.

II

And some cease feeling
Even themselves or for themselves.
Dullness best solves
The tease and doubt of shelling,
And Chance's strange arithmetic
Comes simpler than the reckoning of their shilling.
They keep no check on Armies' decimation.

III

Happy are these who lose imagination:
They have enough to carry with ammunition.
Their spirit drags no pack.
Their old wounds save with cold can not more ache.
Having seen all things red,
Their eyes are rid
Of the hurt of the colour of blood for ever.
And terror's first constriction over,
Their hearts remain small drawn.
Their senses in some scorching cautery of battle
Now long since ironed,
Can laugh among the dying, unconcerned.

IV

Happy the soldier home, with not a notion
How somewhere, every dawn, some men attack,
And many sighs are drained.
Happy the lad whose mind was never trained:
His days are worth forgetting more than not.
He sings along the march
Which we march taciturn, because of dusk,
The long, forlorn, relentless trend
From larger day to huger night.

V

We wise, who with a thought besmirch
Blood over all our soul,
How should we see our task
But through his blunt and lashless eyes?
Alive, he is not vital overmuch;
Dying, not mortal overmuch;
Nor sad, nor proud,
Nor curious at all.
He cannot tell
Old men's placidity from his.

VI

But cursed are dullards whom no cannon stuns,
That they should be as stones.
Wretched are they, and mean
With paucity that never was simplicity.
By choice they made themselves immune

To pity and whatever mourns in man
Before the last sea and the hapless stars;
Whatever mourns when many leave these shores;
Whatever shares
The eternal reciprocity of tears.

Dulce et Decorum Est

Bent double, like old beggars under sacks,
Knock-kneed, coughing like hags, we cursed through sludge,
Till on the haunting flares we turned our backs
And towards our distant rest began to trudge.
Men marched asleep. Many had lost their boots
But limped on, blood-shod. All went lame; all blind;
Drunk with fatigue; deaf even to the hoots
Of gas-shells dropping softly behind.

Gas! GAS! Quick, boys!—An ecstasy of fumbling
Fitting the clumsy helmets just in time,
But someone still was yelling out and stumbling
And flound'ring like a man in fire or lime.—
Dim, through the misty panes and thick green light,
As under a green sea, I saw him drowning.

In all my dreams before my helpless sight
He plunges at me, guttering, choking, drowning.

If in some smothering dreams you too could pace
Behind the wagon that we flung him in,
And watch the white eyes writhing in his face,
His hanging face, like a devil's sick of sin,
If you could hear, at every jolt, the blood
Come gargling from the froth-corrupted lungs,
Bitter as the cud
Of vile, incurable sores on innocent tongues,—
My friend, you would not tell with such high zest
To children ardent for some desperate glory,
The old Lie: *Dulce et decorum est
Pro patria mori.*

The Sentry

We'd found an old Boche dug-out, and he knew,
And gave us hell; for shell on frantic shell
Hammered on top, but never quite burst through.
Rain, guttering down in waterfalls of slime,
Kept slush waist-high and rising hour by hour,
Choked up the steps too thick with clay to climb.

What murk of air remained stank old, and sour
With fumes from whizz-bangs, and the smell of men
Who'd lived there years, and left their curse in the den,
If not their corpses. . . .
                        There we herded from the blast
Of whizz-bangs, but one found our door at last.
Buffeting eyes and breath, snuffing the candles.
And thud! flump! thud! down the steep steps came thumping
And splashing in the flood, deluging muck—
The sentry's body; then, his rifle, handles
Of old Boche bombs, and mud in ruck on ruck.
We dredged him up, for dead, until he whined.
"O sir, my eyes—I'm blind—I'm blind, I'm blind!"
Coaxing, I held a flame against his lids
And said if he could see the least blurred light
He was not blind; in time they'd get all right.
"I can't," he sobbed. Eyeballs, huge-bulged like squids
Watch my dreams still; but I forgot him there
In posting next for duty, and sending a scout
To beg a stretcher somewhere, and floundering about
To other posts under the shrieking air.

Those other wretches, how they bled and spewed,
And one who would have drowned himself for good,—
I try not to remember these things now.
Let dread hark back for one word only: how
Half-listening to that sentry's moans and jumps,
And the wild chattering of his broken teeth,
Renewed most horribly whenever crumps
Pummelled the roof and slogged the air beneath—
Through the dense din, I say, we heard him shout
"I see your lights!" But ours had long died out.

The Dead-Beat

He dropped,—more sullenly than wearily,
Lay stupid like a cod, heavy like meat,
And none of us could kick him to his feet;
Just blinked at my revolver, blearily;
—Didn't appear to know a war was on,
Or see the blasted trench at which he stared.
"I'll do 'em in," he whined. "If this hand's spared,
I'll murder them, I will."

                        A low voice said,
"It's Blighty, p'raps, he sees; his pluck's all gone,
Dreaming of all the valiant, that *aren't* dead;
Bold uncles, smiling ministerially;

Maybe his brave young wife, getting her fun
In some new home, improved materially.
It's not these stiffs have crazed him; nor the Hun."

We sent him down at last, out of the way.
Unwounded;—stout lad, too, before that strafe.
Malingering? Stretcher-bearers winked, "Not half!"

Next day I heard the Doc.'s well-whiskied laugh:
"That scum you sent last night soon died. Hooray!"

Exposure

I

Our brains ache, in the merciless iced east winds that knife us...
Wearied we keep awake because the night is silent...
Low, drooping flares confuse our memory of the salient...
Worried by silence, sentries whisper, curious, nervous,
       But nothing happens.

Watching, we hear the mad gusts tugging on the wire,
Like twitching agonies of men among its brambles.
Northward, incessantly, the flickering gunnery rumbles,
Far off, like a dull rumour of some other war.
       What are we doing here?

The poignant misery of dawn begins to grow...
We only know war lasts, rain soaks, and clouds sag stormy.
Dawn massing in the east her melancholy army
Attacks once more in ranks on shivering ranks of gray,
       But nothing happens.

Sudden successive flights of bullets streak the silence.
Less deadly than the air that shudders black with snow,
With sidelong flowing flakes that flock, pause and renew,
We watch them wandering up and down the wind's nonchalance,
       But nothing happens.

II

Pale flakes with fingering stealth come feeling for our faces—
We cringe in holes, back on forgotten dreams, and stare, snow-dazed,
Deep into grassier ditches. So we drowse, sun-dozed,
Littered with blossoms trickling where the blackbird fusses.
       Is it that we are dying?

Slowly our ghosts drag home: glimpsing the sunk fires, glozed
With crusted dark-red jewels; crickets jingle there;
For hours the innocent mice rejoice: the house is theirs;
Shutters and doors all closed: on us the doors are closed—
        We turn back to our dying.

Since we believe not otherwise can kind fires burn;
Nor ever suns smile true on child, or field, or fruit.
For God's invincible spring our love is made afraid;
Therefore, not loath, we lie out here; therefore were born,
        For love of God seems dying.

Tonight, this frost will fasten on this mud and us,
Shrivelling many hands, puckering foreheads crisp.
The burying-party, picks and shovels in their shaking grasp,
Pause over half-known faces. All their eyes are ice,
        But nothing happens.

Spring Offensive

Halted against the shade of a last hill,
They fed, and, lying easy, were at ease;
And, finding comfortable chests and knees,
Carelessly slept. But many there stood still
To face the stark, blank sky beyond the ridge,
Knowing their feet had come to the end of the world.

Marvelling they stood, and watched the long grass swirled
By the May breeze, murmurous with wasp and midge,
For though the summer oozed into their veins
Like an injected drug for their bones' pains,
Sharp on their souls hung the imminent line of grass,
Fearfully flashed the sky's mysterious glass.

Hour after hour they ponder the warm field—
And the far valley behind, where the buttercups
Had blessed with gold their slow boots coming up,
Where even the little brambles would not yield,
But clutched and clung to them like sorrowing hands;
They breathe like trees unstirred.

Till like a cold gust thrills the little word
At which each body and its soul begird
And tighten them for battle. No alarms
Of bugles, no high flags, no clamorous haste—
Only a lift and flare of eyes that faced
The sun, like a friend with whom their love is done.

O larger shone that smile against the sun,—
Mightier than his whose bounty these have spurned.

So, soon they topped the hill, and raced together
Over an open stretch of herb and heather
Exposed. And instantly the whole sky burned
With fury against them; and soft sudden cups
Opened in thousands for their blood; and the green slopes
Chasmed and steepened sheer to infinite space.
Of them who running on that last high place
Leapt to swift unseen bullets, or went up
On the hot blast and fury of hell's upsurge,
Or plunged and fell away past this world's verge,
Some say God caught them even before they fell.

But what say such as from existence' brink
Ventured but drave too swift to sink,
The few who rushed in the body to enter hell,
And there out-fiending all its fiends and flames
With superhuman inhumanities,
Long-famous glories, immemorial shames—
And crawling slowly back, have by degrees
Regained cool peaceful air in wonder—
Why speak not they of comrades that went under?

The Chances

I mind as 'ow the night before that show
Us five got talkin,—we was in the know.
"Over the top to-morrer; boys, we're for it,
First wave we are, first ruddy wave; that's tore it."
"Ah well," says Jimmy,—an' 'e's seen some scrappin'—
"There ain't no more nor five things as can 'appen,
Ye get knocked out; else wounded—bad or cushy;
Scuppered; or nowt except you're feelin' mushy."

One of us got the knock-out, blown to chops.
T'other was hurt, like, losin' both 'is props.
And one, to use the word of 'ypocrites,
'Ad the misfortune to be took by Fritz.
Now me, I wasn't scratched, praise God Almighty,
(Though next time please I'll thank 'im for a blighty),
But poor old Jim, 'e's livin' an' 'e's not;
'E reckoned 'e'd five chances, an' 'e's 'ad;
'E's wounded, killed, and pris'ner, all the lot—
The ruddy lot all rolled in one. Jim's mad.

S. I. W.

"I will to the King,
  And offer him consolation in his trouble,
  For that man there has set his teeth to die,
  And being one that hates obedience,
  Discipline, and orderliness of life,
  I cannot mourn him."

W. B. YEATS.

Patting goodbye, doubtless they told the lad
He'd always show the Hun a brave man's face;
Father would sooner him dead than in disgrace,-
Was proud to see him going, aye, and glad.
Perhaps his mother whimpered how she'd fret
Until he got a nice, safe wound to nurse.
Sisters would wish girls too could shoot, charge, curse,...
Brothers—would send his favourite cigarette.
Each week, month after month, they wrote the same,
Thinking him sheltered in some Y.M. Hut,
Where once an hour a bullet missed its aim
And misses teased the hunger of his brain.
His eyes grew old with wincing, and his hand
Reckless with ague. Courage leaked, as sand
From the best sandbags after years of rain.
But never leave, wound, fever, trench-foot, shock,
Untrapped the wretch. And death seemed still withheld
For torture of lying machinally shelled,
At the pleasure of this world's Powers who'd run amok.

He'd seen men shoot their hands, on night patrol.
Their people never knew. Yet they were vile.
"Death sooner than dishonour, that's the style!"
So Father said.

                    One dawn, our wire patrol
Carried him. This time, Death had not missed.
We could do nothing but wipe his bleeding cough.
Could it be accident?—Rifles go off...
Not sniped? No. (Later they found the English ball.)
It was the reasoned crisis of his soul.
Against the fires that would not burn him whole
But kept him for death's perjury and scoff
And life's half-promising, and both their riling.

With him they buried the muzzle his teeth had kissed,
And truthfully wrote the Mother, "Tim died smiling."

Futility

Move him into the sun—
Gently its touch awoke him once,
At home, whispering of fields unsown.
Always it woke him, even in France,
Until this morning and this snow.
If anything might rouse him now
The kind old sun will know.

Think how it wakes the seeds—
Woke, once, the clays of a cold star.
Are limbs so dear-achieved, are sides
Full-nerved,—still warm,—too hard to stir?
Was it for this the clay grew tall?
—O what made fatuous sunbeams toil
To break earth's sleep at all?

Smile, Smile, Smile

Head to limp head, the sunk-eyed wounded scanned
Yesterday's Mail; the casualties (typed small)
And (large) Vast Booty from our Latest Haul.
Also, they read of Cheap Homes, not yet planned,
For, said the paper, "when this war is done
The men's first instinct will be making homes.
Meanwhile their foremost need is aerodromes,
It being certain war has but begun.
Peace would do wrong to our undying dead,—
The sons we offered might regret they died
If we got nothing lasting in their stead.
We must be solidly indemnified.
Though all be worthy Victory which all bought,
We rulers sitting in this ancient spot
Would wrong our very selves if we forgot
The greatest glory will be theirs who fought,
Who kept this nation in integrity.
Nation?—The half-limbed readers did not chafe
But smiled at one another curiously
Like secret men who know their secret safe.
This is the thing they know and never speak,
That England one by one had fled to France
(Not many elsewhere now, save under France).
Pictures of these broad smiles appear each week,
And people in whose voice real feeling rings
Say: How they smile! They're happy now, poor things.
September 23, 1918.

Conscious

His fingers wake, and flutter up the bed.
His eyes come open with a pull of will,
Helped by the yellow may-flowers by his head.
The blind-cord drawls across the window-sill . . .
How smooth the floor of the ward is! what a rug!
Who's that talking, somewhere out of sight?
Why are they laughing? What's inside that jug?
"Nurse! Doctor!" "Yes; all right, all right."

But sudden dusk bewilders all the air—
There seems no time to want a drink of water.
Nurse looks so far away. And everywhere
Music and roses burst through crimson slaughter.
Cold; cold; he's cold; and yet so hot:
And there's no light to see the voices by—
No time to dream, and ask—he knows not what.

A Terre

(Being the philosophy of many Soldiers.)

Sit on the bed; I'm blind, and three parts shell.
Be careful; can't shake hands now; never shall.
Both arms have mutinied against me,-brutes.
My fingers fidget like ten idle brats.

I tried to peg out soldierly,—no use!
One dies of war like any old disease.
This bandage feels like pennies on my eyes.
I have my medals?-Discs to make eyes close.
My glorious ribbons?-Ripped from my own back
In scarlet shreds. (That's for your poetry book.)

A short life and a merry one, my brick!
We used to say we'd hate to live dead old,—
Yet now . . . I'd willingly be puffy, bald,
And patriotic. Buffers catch from boys
At least the jokes hurled at them. I suppose
Little I'd ever teach a son, but hitting,
Shooting, war, hunting, all the arts of hurting.
Well, that's what I learnt,—that, and making money.
Your fifty years ahead seem none too many?
Tell me how long I've got? God! For one year
To help myself to nothing more than air!
One Spring! Is one too good to spare, too long?

Spring wind would work its own way to my lung,
And grow me legs as quick as lilac-shoots.
My servant's lamed, but listen how he shouts!
When I'm lugged out, he'll still be good for that.
Here in this mummy-case, you know, I've thought
How well I might have swept his floors for ever.
I'd ask no nights off when the bustle's over,
Enjoying so the dirt. Who's prejudiced
Against a grimed hand when his own's quite dust,
Less live than specks that in the sun-shafts turn,
Less warm than dust that mixes with arms' tan?
I'd love to be a sweep, now, black as Town,
Yes, or a muckman. Must I be his load?
O Life, Life, let me breathe,—a dug-out rat!
Not worse than ours the existences rats lead—
Nosing along at night down some safe rut,
They find a shell-proof home before they rot.
Dead men may envy living mites in cheese,
Or good germs even. Microbes have their joys,
And subdivide, and never come to death,
Certainly flowers have the easiest time on earth.
"I shall be one with nature, herb, and stone."
Shelley would tell me. Shelley would be stunned;
The dullest Tommy hugs that fancy now.
"Pushing up daisies" is their creed, you know.
To grain, then, go my fat, to buds my sap,
For all the usefulness there is in soap.
D'you think the Boche will ever stew man-soup?
Some day, no doubt, if . . .
                          Friend, be very sure
I shall be better off with plants that share
More peaceably the meadow and the shower.
Soft rains will touch me,—as they could touch once,
And nothing but the sun shall make me ware.
Your guns may crash around me. I'll not hear;
Or, if I wince, I shall not know I wince.
Don't take my soul's poor comfort for your jest.
Soldiers may grow a soul when turned to fronds,
But here's the thing's best left at home with friends.

My soul's a little grief, grappling your chest,
To climb your throat on sobs; easily chased
On other sighs and wiped by fresher winds.

Carry my crying spirit till it's weaned
To do without what blood remained these wounds.

Wild With All Regrets

(Another version of "A Terre.")

To SIEGFRIED SASSOON

My arms have mutinied against me—brutes!
My fingers fidget like ten idle brats,
My back's been stiff for hours, damned hours.
Death never gives his squad a Stand-at-ease.
I can't read. There: it's no use. Take your book.
A short life and a merry one, my buck!
We said we'd hate to grow dead old. But now,
Not to live old seems awful: not to renew
My boyhood with my boys, and teach 'em hitting,
Shooting and hunting,—all the arts of hurting!
—Well, that's what I learnt. That, and making money.
Your fifty years in store seem none too many;
But I've five minutes. God! For just two years
To help myself to this good air of yours!
One Spring! Is one too hard to spare? Too long?
Spring air would find its own way to my lung,
And grow me legs as quick as lilac-shoots.

Yes, there's the orderly. He'll change the sheets
When I'm lugged out, oh, couldn't I do that?
Here in this coffin of a bed, I've thought
I'd like to kneel and sweep his floors for ever,—
And ask no nights off when the bustle's over,
For I'd enjoy the dirt; who's prejudiced
Against a grimed hand when his own's quite dust,—
Less live than specks that in the sun-shafts turn?
Dear dust,—in rooms, on roads, on faces' tan!
I'd love to be a sweep's boy, black as Town;
Yes, or a muckman. Must I be his load?
A flea would do. If one chap wasn't bloody,
Or went stone-cold, I'd find another body.

Which I shan't manage now. Unless it's yours.
I shall stay in you, friend, for some few hours.
You'll feel my heavy spirit chill your chest,
And climb your throat on sobs, until it's chased
On sighs, and wiped from off your lips by wind.

I think on your rich breathing, brother, I'll be weaned
To do without what blood remained me from my wound.

December 5, 1917.

Disabled

He sat in a wheeled chair, waiting for dark,
And shivered in his ghastly suit of grey,
Legless, sewn short at elbow. Through the park
Voices of boys rang saddening like a hymn,
Voices of play and pleasure after day,
Till gathering sleep had mothered them from him.

About this time Town used to swing so gay
When glow-lamps budded in the light blue trees,
And girls glanced lovelier as the air grew dim,
—In the old times, before he threw away his knees.
Now he will never feel again how slim
Girls' waists are, or how warm their subtle hands.
All of them touch him like some queer disease.

There was an artist silly for his face,
For it was younger than his youth, last year.
Now, he is old; his back will never brace;
He's lost his colour very far from here,
Poured it down shell-holes till the veins ran dry,
And half his lifetime lapsed in the hot race,
And leap of purple spurted from his thigh.
One time he liked a bloodsmear down his leg,
After the matches carried shoulder-high.
It was after football, when he'd drunk a peg,
He thought he'd better join. He wonders why . . .
Someone had said he'd look a god in kilts.

That's why; and maybe, too, to please his Meg,
Aye, that was it, to please the giddy jilts,
He asked to join. He didn't have to beg;
Smiling they wrote his lie; aged nineteen years.
Germans he scarcely thought of; and no fears
Of Fear came yet. He thought of jewelled hilts
For daggers in plaid socks; of smart salutes;
And care of arms; and leave; and pay arrears;
Esprit de corps; and hints for young recruits.
And soon, he was drafted out with drums and cheers.
Some cheered him home, but not as crowds cheer Goal.
Only a solemn man who brought him fruits
Thanked him; and then inquired about his soul.
Now, he will spend a few sick years in Institutes,
And do what things the rules consider wise,
And take whatever pity they may dole.
To-night he noticed how the women's eyes

Passed from him to the strong men that were whole.
How cold and late it is! Why don't they come
And put him into bed? Why don't they come?

The End

After the blast of lightning from the east,
The flourish of loud clouds, the Chariot throne,
After the drums of time have rolled and ceased
And from the bronze west long retreat is blown,

Shall Life renew these bodies? Of a truth
All death will he annul, all tears assuage?
Or fill these void veins full again with youth
And wash with an immortal water age?

When I do ask white Age, he saith not so,—
"My head hangs weighed with snow."
And when I hearken to the Earth she saith
"My fiery heart sinks aching. It is death.
Mine ancient scars shall not be glorified
Nor my titanic tears the seas be dried."

THE WAR POEMS OF SIEGFRIED SASSOON

Dans la trêve désolée de cette matinée, ces hommes qui avaient été tenaillés par la fatigue, fouettés par la pluie, bouleversés par toute une nuit de tonnerre, ces rescapés des volcans et de l'inondation entrevoyaient à quel point la guerre, aussi hideuse au moral qu'au physique, non seulement viole le bon sens, avilit les grandes idées, commande tous les crimes—mais ils se rappelaient combien elle avait développé en eux et autour d'eux tous les mauvais instincts sans en excepter un seul; la méchanceté jusqu'au sadisme, l'égoïsme jusqu'à la férocité, le besoin de jouir jusqu'à la folie.

HENRI BARBUSSE.
(Le Feu.)

I

Prelude: The Troops

Dim, gradual thinning of the shapeless gloom
Shudders to drizzling daybreak that reveals
Disconsolate men who stamp their sodden boots
And turn dulled, sunken faces to the sky
Haggard and hopeless. They, who have beaten down
The stale despair of night, must now renew
Their desolation in the truce of dawn,
Murdering the livid hours that grope for peace.

Yet these, who cling to life with stubborn hands,
Can grin through storms of death and find a gap
In the clawed, cruel tangles of his defence.
They march from safety, and the bird-sung joy
Of grass-green thickets, to the land where all
Is ruin, and nothing blossoms but the sky
That hastens over them where they endure
Sad, smoking, flat horizons, reeking woods,
And foundered trench-lines volleying doom for doom.

O my brave brown companions, when your souls
Flock silently away, and the eyeless dead,
Shame the wild beast of battle on the ridge,
Death will stand grieving in that field of war
Since your unvanquished hardihood is spent.
And through some mooned Valhalla there will pass
Battalions and battalions, scarred from hell;
The unreturning army that was youth;
The legions who have suffered and are dust.

Dreamers

Soldiers are citizens of death's gray land,
    Drawing no dividend from time's to-morrows.
In the great hour of destiny they stand,
    Each with his feuds, and jealousies, and sorrows.
Soldiers are sworn to action; they must win
    Some flaming, fatal climax with their lives.
Soldiers are dreamers; when the guns begin
    They think of firelit homes, clean beds, and wives.

I see them in foul dug-outs, gnawed by rats,
    And in the ruined trenches, lashed with rain,
Dreaming of things they did with balls and bats,
    And mocked by hopeless longing to regain
Bank-holidays, and picture shows, and spats,
    And going to the office in the train.

The Redeemer

Darkness: the rain sluiced down; the mire was deep;
It was past twelve on a mid-winter night,
When peaceful folk in beds lay snug asleep:
There, with much work to do before the light,
We lugged our clay-sucked boots as best we might
Along the trench; sometimes a bullet sang,
And droning shells burst with a hollow bang;

We were soaked, chilled and wretched, every one.
Darkness: the distant wink of a huge gun.

I turned in the black ditch, loathing the storm;
A rocket fizzed and burned with blanching flare,
And lit the face of what had been a form
Floundering in mirk. He stood before me there;
I say that he was Christ; stiff in the glare,
And leaning forward from his burdening task,
Both arms supporting it; his eyes on mine
Stared from the woeful head that seemed a mask
Of mortal pain in Hell's unholy shine.

No thorny crown, only a woollen cap
He wore—an English soldier, white and strong,
Who loved his time like any simple chap,
Good days of work and sport and homely song;
Now he has learned that nights are very long,
And dawn a watching of the windowed sky.
But to the end, unjudging, he'll endure
Horror and pain, not uncontent to die
That Lancaster on Lune may stand secure.

He faced me, reeling in his weariness,
Shouldering his load of planks, so hard to bear.
I say that he was Christ, who wrought to bless
All groping things with freedom bright as air,
And with His mercy washed and made them fair.
Then the flame sank, and all grew black as pitch,
While we began to struggle along the ditch;
And some one flung his burden in the muck,
Mumbling: "O Christ Almighty, now I'm stuck!"

Trench Duty

Shaken from sleep, and numbed and scarce awake,
Out in the trench with three hours' watch to take,
I blunder through the splashing mirk; and then
Hear the gruff muttering voices of the men
Crouching in cabins candle-chinked with light.
Hark! There's the big bombardment on our right
Rumbling and bumping; and the dark's a glare
Of flickering horror in the sectors where
We raid the Boche; men waiting, stiff and chilled,
Or crawling on their bellies through the wire.
"What? Stretcher-bearers wanted? Some one killed?"
Five minutes ago I heard a sniper fire:
Why did he do it? . . . Starlight overhead—

Blank stars. I'm wide-awake; and some chap's dead.

Wirers

"Pass it along, the wiring party's going out"—
And yawning sentries mumble, "Wirers going out."
Unravelling; twisting; hammering stakes with muffled thud,
They toil with stealthy haste and anger in their blood.

The Boche sends up a flare. Black forms stand rigid there,
Stock-still like posts; then darkness, and the clumsy ghosts
Stride hither and thither, whispering, tripped by clutching snare
Of snags and tangles.
Ghastly dawn with vaporous coasts
Gleams desolate along the sky, night's misery ended.

Young Hughes was badly hit; I heard him carried away,
Moaning at every lurch; no doubt he'll die to-day.
But *we* can say the front-line wire's been safely mended.

Break of Day

There seemed a smell of autumn in the air
At the bleak end of night; he shivered there
In a dank, musty dug-out where he lay,
Legs wrapped in sand-bags,—lumps of chalk and clay
Spattering his face. Dry-mouthed, he thought, "To-day
We start the damned attack; and, Lord knows why,
Zero's at nine; how bloody if I'm done in
Under the freedom of that morning sky!"
And then he coughed and dozed, cursing the din.

Was it the ghost of autumn in that smell
Of underground, or God's blank heart grown kind,
That sent a happy dream to him in hell?—
Where men are crushed like clods, and crawl to find
Some crater for their wretchedness; who lie
In outcast immolation, doomed to die
Far from clean things or any hope of cheer,
Cowed anger in their eyes, till darkness brims
And roars into their heads, and they can hear
Old childish talk, and tags of foolish hymns.

He sniffs the chilly air; (his dreaming starts).
He's riding in a dusty Sussex lane
In quiet September; slowly night departs;
And he's a living soul, absolved from pain.
Beyond the brambled fences where he goes

Are glimmering fields with harvest piled in sheaves,
And tree-tops dark against the stars grown pale;
Then, clear and shrill, a distant farm-cock crows;
And there's a wall of mist along the vale
Where willows shake their watery-sounding leaves.
He gazes on it all, and scarce believes
That earth is telling its old peaceful tale;
He thanks the blessed world that he was born . . .
Then, far away, a lonely note of the horn.

They're drawing the Big Wood! Unlatch the gate,
And set Golumpus going on the grass:
He knows the corner where it's best to wait
And hear the crashing woodland chorus pass;
The corner where old foxes make their track
To the Long Spinney; that's the place to be.
The bracken shakes below an ivied tree,
And then a cub looks out; and "Tally-o-back!"
He bawls, and swings his thong with volleying crack,—
All the clean thrill of autumn in his blood,
And hunting surging through him like a flood
In joyous welcome from the untroubled past;
While the war drifts away, forgotten at last.

Now a red, sleepy sun above the rim
Of twilight stares along the quiet weald,
And the kind, simple country shines revealed
In solitudes of peace, no longer dim.
The old horse lifts his face and thanks the light,
Then stretches down his head to crop the green.
All things that he has loved are in his sight;
The places where his happiness has been
Are in his eyes, his heart, and they are good.

* * * * *

Hark! there's the horn: they're drawing the Big Wood.

A Working Party

Three hours ago he blundered up the trench,
Sliding and poising, groping with his boots;
Sometimes he tripped and lurched against the walls
With hands that pawed the sodden bags of chalk.
He couldn't see the man who walked in front;
Only he heard the drum and rattle of feet
Stepping along the trench-boards,—often splashing
Wretchedly where the sludge was ankle-deep.

Voices would grunt, "Keep to your right,—make way!"
When squeezing past the men from the front-line:
White faces peered, puffing a point of red;
Candles and braziers glinted through the chinks
And curtain-flaps of dug-outs; then the gloom
Swallowed his sense of sight; he stooped and swore
Because a sagging wire had caught his neck.
A flare went up; the shining whiteness spread
And flickered upward, showing nimble rats,
And mounds of glimmering sand-bags, bleached with rain;
Then the slow, silver moment died in dark.

The wind came posting by with chilly gusts
And buffeting at corners, piping thin
And dreary through the crannies; rifle-shots
Would split and crack and sing along the night,
And shells came calmly through the drizzling air
To burst with hollow bang below the hill.

Three hours ago he stumbled up the trench;
Now he will never walk that road again:
He must be carried back, a jolting lump
Beyond all need of tenderness and care;
A nine-stone corpse with nothing more to do.

He was a young man with a meagre wife
And two pale children in a Midland town;
He showed the photograph to all his mates;
And they considered him a decent chap
Who did his work and hadn't much to say,
And always laughed at other people's jokes
Because he hadn't any of his own.

That night, when he was busy at his job
Of piling bags along the parapet,
He thought how slow time went, stamping his feet,
And blowing on his fingers, pinched with cold.

He thought of getting back by half-past twelve,
And tot of rum to send him warm to sleep
In draughty dug-out frowsty with the fumes
Of coke, and full of snoring, weary men.

He pushed another bag along the top,
Craning his body outward; then a flare
Gave one white glimpse of No Man's Land and wire;
And as he dropped his head the instant split
His startled life with lead, and all went out.

Stand-To: Good Friday Morning

I'd been on duty from two till four.
I went and stared at the dug-out door.
Down in the frowst I heard them snore.
"Stand-to!" Somebody grunted and swore.
    Dawn was misty; the skies were still;
    Larks were singing, discordant, shrill;
    They seemed happy; but *I* felt ill.
Deep in water I splashed my way
Up the trench to our bogged front line.
Rain had fallen the whole damned night.
O Jesus, send me a wound to-day,
And I'll believe in Your bread and wine,
And get my bloody old sins washed white!

"In the Pink"

So Davies wrote: "This leaves me in the pink."
Then scrawled his name: "Your loving sweetheart, Willie."
With crosses for a hug. He'd had a drink
Of rum and tea; and, though the barn was chilly,
For once his blood ran warm; he had pay to spend.
Winter was passing; soon the year would mend.

He couldn't sleep that night. Stiff in the dark
He groaned and thought of Sundays at the farm,
When he'd go out as cheerful as a lark
In his best suit to wander arm-in-arm
With brown-eyed Gwen, and whisper in her ear
The simple, silly things she liked to hear.

And then he thought: to-morrow night we trudge
Up to the trenches, and my boots are rotten.
Five miles of stodgy clay and freezing sludge,
And everything but wretchedness forgotten.
To-night he's in the pink; but soon he'll die.
And still the war goes on; *he* don't know why.

The Hero

"Jack fell as he'd have wished," the Mother said,
And folded up the letter that she'd read.
"The Colonel writes so nicely." Something broke
In the tired voice that quavered to a choke.
She half looked up. "We mothers are so proud
Of our dead soldiers." Then her face was bowed.

Quietly the Brother Officer went out.
He'd told the poor old dear some gallant lies
That she would nourish all her days, no doubt.
For while he coughed and mumbled, her weak eyes
Had shone with gentle triumph, brimmed with joy,
Because he'd been so brave, her glorious boy.

He thought how "Jack," cold-footed, useless swine,
Had panicked down the trench that night the mine
Went up at Wicked Corner; how he'd tried
To get sent home; and how, at last, he died,
Blown to small bits. And no one seemed to care
Except that lonely woman with white hair.

Before the Battle

Music of whispering trees
Hushed by the broad-winged breeze
Where shaken water gleams;
And evening radiance falling
With reedy bird-notes calling.
O bear me safe through dark, you low-voiced streams.

I have no need to pray
That fear may pass away;
I scorn the growl and rumble of the fight
That summons me from cool
Silence of marsh and pool,
And yellow lilies islanded in light.
O river of stars and shadows, lead me through the night.

June 25, 1916.

The Road

The road is thronged with women; soldiers pass
And halt, but never see them; yet they're here—
A patient crowd along the sodden grass,
Silent, worn out with waiting, sick with fear.

The road goes crawling up a long hillside,
All ruts and stones and sludge, and the emptied dregs
Of battle thrown in heaps. Here where they died
Are stretched big-bellied horses with stiff legs;
And dead men, bloody-fingered from the fight,
Stare up at caverned darkness winking white.

You in the bomb-scorched kilt, poor sprawling Jock,
You tottered here and fell, and stumbled on,
Half dazed for want of sleep. No dream could mock
Your reeling brain with comforts lost and gone.
You did not feel her arms about your knees,
Her blind caress, her lips upon your head:
Too tired for thoughts of home and love and ease,
The road would serve you well enough for bed.

Two Hundred Years After

Trudging by Corbie Ridge one winter's night,
(Unless old, hearsay memories tricked his sight),
Along the pallid edge of the quiet sky
He watched a nosing lorry grinding on,
And straggling files of men; when these were gone,
A double limber and six mules went by,
Hauling the rations up through ruts and mud
To trench-lines digged two hundred years ago.
Then darkness hid them with a rainy scud,
And soon he saw the village lights below.

But when he'd told his tale, an old man said
That *he'd* seen soldiers pass along that hill;
"Poor, silent things, they were the English dead
Who came to fight in France and got their fill."

The Dream

I

Moonlight and dew-drenched blossom, and the scent
Of summer gardens; these can bring you all
Those dreams that in the starlit silence fall:
Sweet songs are full of odours.
                              While I went
Last night in drizzling dusk along a lane,
I passed a squalid farm; from byre and midden
Came the rank smell that brought me once again
A dream of war that in the past was hidden.

II

Up a disconsolate straggling village street
I saw the tired troops trudge: I heard their feet.
The cheery Q.M.S. was there to meet
And guide our Company in . . .
                              I watched them stumble.
Into some crazy hovel, too beat to grumble;
Saw them file inward, slipping from their backs
Rifles, equipment, packs.

On filthy straw they sit in the gloom, each face
Bowed to patched, sodden boots they must unlace,
While the wind chills their sweat through chinks and cracks.

III

I'm looking at their blistered feet; young Jones
Stares up at me, mud-splashed and white and jaded;
Out of his eyes the morning light has faded.
Old soldiers with three winters in their bones
Puff their damp Woodbines, whistle, stretch their toes
They can still grin at me, for each of 'em knows
That I'm as tired as they are . . .
                              Can they guess
The secret burden that is always mine?—
Pride in their courage; pity for their distress;
And burning bitterness
That I must take them to the accursèd Line.

IV

I cannot hear their voices, but I see
Dim candles in the barn: they gulp their tea,
And soon they'll sleep like logs. Ten miles away
The battle winks and thuds in blundering strife.
And I must lead them nearer, day by day,
To the foul beast of war that bludgeons life.

At Carnoy

Down in the hollow there's the whole Brigade
Camped in four groups: through twilight falling slow
I hear a sound of mouth-organs, ill-played,
And murmur of voices, gruff, confused, and low.
Crouched among thistle-tufts I've watched the glow
Of a blurred orange sunset flare and fade;

And I'm content. To-morrow we must go
To take some cursèd Wood. . . . O world God made!

July 3, 1916.

Battalion Relief

"*Fall in! Now, get a move on!*" (Curse the rain.)
We splash away along the straggling village,
Out to the flat rich country green with June . . .
And sunset flares across wet crops and tillage,
Blazing with splendour-patches. Harvest soon
Up in the Line. "*Perhaps the War'll be done
By Christmas-time. Keep smiling then, old son!*"

Here's the Canal: it's dusk; we cross the bridge.
"*Lead on there by platoons.*" The Line's a-glare
With shell-fire through the poplars; distant rattle
Of rifles and machine-guns. "*Fritz is there!
Christ, ain't it lively, Sergeant? Is't a battle?*"
More rain: the lightning blinks, and thunder rumbles.
"There's overhead artillery," some chap grumbles.

"*What's all this mob, by the cross-road?*" (The guides) . . .
"*Lead on with Number One.*" (And off they go.)

"*Three-minute intervals.*" . . . Poor blundering files,
Sweating and blindly burdened; who's to know
If death will catch them in those two dark miles?
(More rain.) "*Lead on, Headquarters.*"
                                (That's the lot.)
"*Who's that? O, Sergeant-major; don't get shot!
And tell me, have we won this war or not?*"

The Dug-Out

Why do you lie with your legs ungainly huddled,
And one arm bent across your sullen cold
Exhausted face? It hurts my heart to watch you,
Deep-shadow'd from the candle's guttering gold;
And you wonder why I shake you by the shoulder;
Drowsy, you mumble and sigh and turn your head . . .
*You are too young to fall asleep for ever;
And when you sleep you remind me of the dead.*

The Rear-Guard

(Hindenburg Line, April 1917.)

Groping along the tunnel, step by step,
He winked his prying torch with patching glare
From side to side, and sniffed the unwholesome air.

Tins, boxes, bottles, shapes too vague to know,
A mirror smashed, the mattress from a bed;
And he, exploring fifty feet below
The rosy gloom of battle overhead.

Tripping, he grabbed the wall; saw some one lie
Humped at his feet, half-hidden by a rug,
And stooped to give the sleeper's arm a tug.
"I'm looking for headquarters." No reply.
"God blast your neck!" (For days he'd had no sleep,)
"Get up and guide me through this stinking place."
Savage, he kicked a soft, unanswering heap,
And flashed his beam across the livid face
Terribly glaring up, whose eyes yet wore
Agony dying hard ten days before;
And fists of fingers clutched a blackening wound.

Alone he staggered on until he found
Dawn's ghost that filtered down a shafted stair
To the dazed, muttering creatures underground
Who hear the boom of shells in muffled sound.
At last, with sweat of horror in his hair,
He climbed through darkness to the twilight air,
Unloading hell behind him step by step.

I Stood With the Dead

I stood with the Dead, so forsaken and still:
    When dawn was grey I stood with the Dead.
And my slow heart said, "You must kill; you must kill:
    Soldier, soldier, morning is red."

On the shapes of the slain in their crumpled disgrace
    I stared for a while through the thin cold rain. . . .
"O lad that I loved, there is rain on your face,
    And your eyes are blurred and sick like the plain."

I stood with the Dead. . . . They were dead; they were dead;
   My heart and my head beat a march of dismay;
And gusts of the wind came dulled by the guns . . .
   "Fall in!" I shouted; "Fall in for your pay!"

Suicide in Trenches

I knew a simple soldier boy
Who grinned at life in empty joy,
Slept soundly through the lonesome dark,
And whistled early with the lark.

In winter trenches, cowed and glum
With crumps and lice and lack of rum,
He put a bullet through his brain.
No one spoke of him again.

                         * * * * *

You smug-faced crowds with kindling eye
Who cheer when soldier lads march by,
Sneak home and pray you'll never know
The hell where youth and laughter go.

Attack

At dawn the ridge emerges massed and dun
In the wild purple of the glowering sun
Smouldering through spouts of drifting smoke that shroud
The menacing scarred slope; and, one by one,
Tanks creep and topple forward to the wire.
The barrage roars and lifts. Then, clumsily bowed
With bombs and guns and shovels and battle-gear,
Men jostle and climb to meet the bristling fire.
Lines of grey, muttering faces, masked with fear,
They leave their trenches, going over the top,
While time ticks blank and busy on their wrists,
And hope, with furtive eyes and grappling fists,
Flounders in mud. O Jesu, make it stop!

Counter-Attack

We'd gained our first objective hours before
While dawn broke like a face with blinking eyes,
Pallid, unshaved and thirsty, blind with smoke.
Things seemed all right at first. We held their line,
With bombers posted, Lewis guns well placed,

And clink of shovels deepening the shallow trench.
The place was rotten with dead; green clumsy legs
High-booted, sprawled and grovelled along the saps
And trunks, face downward in the sucking mud,
Wallowed like trodden sand-bags loosely filled;
And naked sodden buttocks, mats of hair,
Bulged, clotted heads, slept in the plastering slime.
And then the rain began,—the jolly old rain!

A yawning soldier knelt against the bank,
Staring across the morning blear with fog;
He wondered when the Allemands would get busy;
And then, of course, they started with five-nines
Traversing, sure as fate, and never a dud.
Mute in the clamour of shells he watched them burst
Spouting dark earth and wire with gusts from hell,
While posturing giants dissolved in drifts of smoke.

He crouched and flinched, dizzy with galloping fear,
Sick for escape,—loathing the strangled horror
And butchered, frantic gestures of the dead.

An officer came blundering down the trench:
"Stand-to and man the fire-step!" On he went . . .
Gasping and bawling, "Fire-step . . . counter-attack!"
Then the haze lifted. Bombing on the right
Down the old sap: machine-guns on the left;
And stumbling figures looming out in front.
"O Christ, they're coming at us!" Bullets spat,
And he remembered his rifle . . . rapid fire . . .
And started blazing wildly . . . then a bang
Crumpled and spun him sideways, knocked him out
To grunt and wriggle: none heeded him; he choked
And fought the flapping veils of smothering gloom,
Lost in a blurred confusion of yells and groans . . .
Down, and down, and down, he sank and drowned,
Bleeding to death. The counter-attack had failed.

The Effect

"The effect of our bombardment was terrific. One man told me he had never
seen so many dead before."

War Correspondent.

"*He'd never seen so many dead before.*"
They sprawled in yellow daylight while he swore
And gasped and lugged his everlasting load
Of bombs along what once had been a road.

"How peaceful are the dead."
Who put that silly gag in some one's head?

"He'd never seen so many dead before."
The lilting words danced up and down his brain,
While corpses jumped and capered in the rain.
No, no; he wouldn't count them any more . . .
The dead have done with pain:
They've choked; they can't come back to life again.

When Dick was killed last week he looked like that,
Flapping along the fire-step like a fish,
After the blazing crump had knocked him flat . . .
"How many dead? As many as ever you wish.
Don't count 'em; they're too many.
Who'll buy my nice fresh corpses, two a penny?"

Remorse

Lost in the swamp and welter of the pit,
He flounders off the duck-boards; only he knows
Each flash and spouting crash,—each instant lit
When gloom reveals the streaming rain. He goes
Heavily, blindly on. And, while he blunders,
"Could anything be worse than this?"—he wonders,
Remembering how he saw those Germans run,
Screaming for mercy among the stumps of trees:
Green-faced, they dodged and darted: there was one
Livid with terror, clutching at his knees . . .
Our chaps were sticking 'em like pigs. . . . "O hell!"
He thought—"there's things in war one dare not tell
Poor father sitting safe at home, who reads
Of dying heroes and their deathless deeds."

In an Underground Dressing-Station

Quietly they set their burden down: he tried
To grin; moaned; moved his head from side to side.

* * * * *

He gripped the stretcher; stiffened; glared; and screamed,
"O put my leg down, doctor, do!" (He'd got
A bullet in his ankle; and he'd been shot
Horribly through the guts.) The surgeon seemed
So kind and gentle, saying, above that crying,
"You *must* keep still, my lad." But he was dying.

Died of Wounds

His wet, white face and miserable eyes
Brought nurses to him more than groans and sighs:
But hoarse and low and rapid rose and fell
His troubled voice: he did the business well.

The ward grew dark; but he was still complaining,
And calling out for "Dickie." "Curse the Wood!
It's time to go; O Christ, and what's the good?—
We'll never take it; and it's always raining."

I wondered where he'd been; then heard him shout,
"They snipe like hell! O Dickie, don't go out" . . .
I fell asleep . . . next morning he was dead;
And some Slight Wound lay smiling on his bed.

II

"*They*"

The Bishop tells us: "When the boys come back
They will not be the same; for they'll have fought
In a just cause: they lead the last attack
On Anti-Christ; their comrade's blood has bought
New right to breed an honourable race.
They have challenged Death and dared him face to face."

"We're none of us the same!" the boys reply.
"For George lost both his legs; and Bill's stone blind;
Poor Jim's shot through the lungs and like to die;
And Bert's gone syphilitic: you'll not find
A chap who's served that hasn't found *some* change."
And the Bishop said; "The ways of God are strange!"

Base Details

If I were fierce, and bald, and short of breath,
    I'd live with scarlet Majors at the Base,
And speed glum heroes up the line to death.
    You'd see me with my puffy petulant face,
Guzzling and gulping in the best hotel,
    Reading the Roll of Honour. "Poor young chap,"
I'd say—"I used to know his father well;
    Yes, we've lost heavily in this last scrap."
And when the war is done and youth stone dead,
I'd toddle safely home and die—in bed.

Lamentations

I found him in a guard-room at the Base.
From the blind darkness I had heard his crying
And blundered in. With puzzled, patient face
A sergeant watched him; it was no good trying
To stop it; for he howled and beat his chest.
And, all because his brother had gone West,
Raved at the bleeding war; his rampant grief
Moaned, shouted, sobbed, and choked, while he was kneeling
Half-naked on the floor. In my belief
Such men have lost all patriotic feeling.

The General

"Good-morning; good-morning!" the General said
When we met him last week on our way to the Line,
Now the soldiers he smiled at are most of 'em dead,
And we're cursing his staff for incompetent swine.
"He's a cheery old card," grunted Harry to Jack
As they slogged up to Arras with rifle and pack.

* * * * *

But he did for them both by his plan of attack.

How to Die

Dark clouds are smouldering into red
    While down the craters morning burns.
The dying soldier shifts his head
    To watch the glory that returns:
He lifts his fingers toward the skies
    Where holy brightness breaks in flame;
Radiance reflected in his eyes,
    And on his lips a whispered name.

You'd think, to hear some people talk,
    That lads go West with sobs and curses,
And sullen faces white as chalk,
    Hankering for wreaths and tombs and hearses.
But they've been taught the way to do it
    Like Christian soldiers; not with haste
And shuddering groans; but passing through it
    With due regard for decent taste.

Editorial Impression

He seemed so certain "all was going well,"
As he discussed the glorious time he'd had
While visiting the trenches.
                                    "One can tell
You've gathered big impressions!" grinned the lad
Who'd been severely wounded in the back
In some wiped-out impossible Attack.
"Impressions? Yes, most vivid! I am writing
A little book called *Europe on the Rack*,
Based on notes made while witnessing the fighting.
I hope I've caught the feeling of 'the Line,'
And the amazing spirit of the troops.
By Jove, those flying-chaps of ours are fine!
I watched one daring beggar looping loops,
Soaring and diving like some bird of prey.
And through it all I felt that splendour shine
Which makes us win."
                                    The soldier sipped his wine.
"Ah, yes, but it's the Press that leads the way!"

Fight to a Finish

The boys came back. Bands played and flags were flying,
    And Yellow-Pressmen thronged the sunlit street
To cheer the soldiers who'd refrained from dying,
    And hear the music of returning feet.
"Of all the thrills and ardours War has brought,
This moment is the finest." (So they thought.)

Snapping their bayonets on to charge the mob,
    Grim Fusiliers broke ranks with glint of steel.
At last the boys had found a cushy job.

* * * * *

I heard the Yellow-Pressmen grunt and squeal;
And with my trusty bombers turned and went
To clear those Junkers out of Parliament.

Atrocities

You told me, in your drunken-boasting mood,
How once you butchered prisoners. That was good!
I'm sure you felt no pity while they stood
Patient and cowed and scared, as prisoners should.

How did you do them in? Come, don't be shy:
You know I love to hear how Germans die,
Downstairs in dug-outs. "Camerad!" they cry;
Then squeal like stoats when bombs begin to fly.

* * * * *

And you? I know your record. You went sick
When orders looked unwholesome: then, with trick
And lie, you wangled home. And here you are,
Still talking big and boozing in a bar.

The Fathers

Snug at the club two fathers sat,
Gross, goggle-eyed, and full of chat.
One of them said: "My eldest lad
Writes cheery letters from Bagdad.
But Arthur's getting all the fun
At Arras with his nine-inch gun."

"Yes," wheezed the other, "that's the luck!
My boy's quite broken-hearted, stuck
In England training all this year.
Still, if there's truth in what we hear,
The Huns intend to ask for more
    Before they bolt across the Rhine."
I watched them toddle through the door—
    These impotent old friends of mine.

"Blighters"

The house is crammed: tier beyond tier they grin
And cackle at the Show, while prancing ranks
Of harlots shrill the chorus, drunk with din;
"We're sure the Kaiser loves the dear old Tanks!"

I'd like to see a Tank come down the stalls,
Lurching to rag-time tunes, or "Home, sweet Home,"—
And there'd be no more jokes in Music-halls
To mock the riddled corpses round Bapaume.

Glory of Women

You love us when we're heroes, home on leave,
Or wounded in a mentionable place.
You worship decorations; you believe
That chivalry redeems the war's disgrace.
You make us shells. You listen with delight,
By tales of dirt and danger fondly thrilled.
You crown our distant ardours while we fight,
And mourn our laurelled memories when we're killed.

You can't believe that British troops "retire"
When hell's last horror breaks them, and they run,
Trampling the terrible corpses—blind with blood.
O German mother dreaming by the fire,
While you are knitting socks to send your son
His face is trodden deeper in the mud.

Their Frailty

He's got a Blighty wound. He's safe; and then
    War's fine and bold and bright.
She can forget the doomed and prisoned men
    Who agonize and fight.

He's back in France. She loathes the listless strain
    And peril of his plight.
Beseeching Heaven to send him home again,
    She prays for peace each night.

Husbands and sons and lovers; everywhere
    They die; War bleeds us white.
Mothers and wives and sweethearts,—they don't care
    So long as He's all right.

Does It Matter?

Does it matter?—losing your legs? . . .
For people will always be kind,
And you need not show that you mind
When the others come in after football
To gobble their muffins and eggs.

Does it matter?—losing your sight? . . .
There's such splendid work for the blind;
And people will always be kind,
As you sit on the terrace remembering
And turning your face to the light.

Do they matter?—those dreams from the pit? . . .
You can drink and forget and be glad,
And people won't say that you're mad;
For they'll know that you've fought for your country,
And no one will worry a bit.

Survivors

No doubt they'll soon get well; the shock and strain
Have caused their stammering, disconnected talk.
Of course they're "longing to go out again,"—
These boys with old, scared faces, learning to walk,
They'll soon forget their haunted nights; their cowed
Subjection to the ghosts of friends who died,—
Their dreams that drip with murder; and they'll be proud
Of glorious war that shatter'd all their pride . . .
Men who went out to battle, grim and glad;
Children, with eyes that hate you, broken and mad.

CRAIGLOCKHART, *Oct.* 1917.

Joy-Bells

Ring your sweet bells; but let them be farewells
    To the green-vista'd gladness of the past
That changed us into soldiers; swing your bells
    To a joyful chime; but let it be the last.

What means this metal in windy belfries hung
    When guns are all our need? Dissolve these bells
Whose tones are tuned for peace: with martial tongue
    Let them cry doom and storm the sun with shells.

Bells are like fierce-browed prelates who proclaim
    That "if our Lord returned He'd fight for *us*."
So let our bells and bishops do the same,
    Shoulder to shoulder with the motor-bus.

Arms and the Man

Young Croesus went to pay his call
On Colonel Sawbones, Caxton Hall:
And, though his wound was healed and mended,
He hoped he'd get his leave extended.

The waiting-room was dark and bare.
He eyed a neat-framed notice there
Above the fireplace hung to show
Disabled heroes where to go
For arms and legs; with scale of price,
And words of dignified advice
How officers could get them free.

Elbow or shoulder, hip or knee,—
Two arms, two legs, though all were lost,
They'd be restored him free of cost.

Then a Girl-Guide looked in to say,
"Will Captain Croesus come this way?"

When I'm Among a Blaze of Lights . . .

When I'm among a blaze of lights,
With tawdry music and cigars
And women dawdling through delights,
And officers at cocktail bars,—
Sometimes I think of garden nights
And elm trees nodding at the stars.

I dream of a small firelit room
With yellow candles burning straight,
And glowing pictures in the gloom,
And kindly books that hold me late.
Of things like these I love to think
When I can never be alone:
Then some one says, "Another drink?"—
And turns my living heart to stone.

The Kiss

To these I turn, in these I trust;
Brother Lead and Sister Steel.
To his blind power I make appeal;
I guard her beauty clean from rust.

He spins and burns and loves the air,
And splits a skull to win my praise;
But up the nobly marching days
She glitters naked, cold and fair.

Sweet Sister, grant your soldier this;
That in good fury he may feel
The body where he sets his heel
Quail from your downward darting kiss.

The Tombstone-Maker

He primmed his loose red mouth, and leaned his head
Against a sorrowing angel's breast, and said:
"You'd think so much bereavement would have made
Unusual big demands upon my trade.
The War comes cruel hard on some poor folk—
Unless the fighting stops I'll soon be broke."

He eyed the Cemetery across the road—
"There's scores of bodies out abroad, this while,
That should be here by rights; they little know'd
How they'd get buried in such wretched style."

I told him, with a sympathetic grin,
That Germans boil dead soldiers down for fat;
And he was horrified. "What shameful sin!
O sir, that Christian men should come to that!"

The One-Legged Man

Propped on a stick he viewed the August weald;
Squat orchard trees and oasts with painted cowls;
A homely, tangled hedge, a corn-stooked field,
With sound of barking dogs and farmyard fowls.

And he'd come home again to find it more
Desirable than ever it was before.
How right it seemed that he should reach the span
Of comfortable years allowed to man!

Splendid to eat and sleep and choose a wife,
Safe with his wound, a citizen of life.
He hobbled blithely through the garden gate,
And thought; "Thank God they had to amputate!"

Return of the Heroes

A lady watches from the crowd,
Enthusiastic, flushed, and proud.

"Oh! there's Sir Henry Dudster! Such a splendid leader!
How pleased he looks! What rows of ribbons on his tunic!
Such dignity . . . Saluting . . . (*Wave your flag . . . now, Freda!*) . . .
Yes, dear, I saw a Prussian General once,—at Munich.

"Here's the next carriage! . . . Jack was once in Leggit's Corps;
That's him! . . . I think the stout one is Sir Godfrey Stoomer.
They *must* feel sad to know they can't win any more
Great victories! . . . Aren't they glorious men? . . . so full of humour!"

III

Twelve Months After

Hullo! here's my platoon, the lot I had last year.
"The War'll be over soon."
                     "What 'opes?"
                     "No bloody fear!"
Then, "Number Seven, 'shun! All present and correct."
They're standing in the sun, impassive and erect.
Young Gibson with his grin; and Morgan, tired and white;
Jordan, who's out to win a D.C.M. some night:
And Hughes that's keen on wiring; and Davies ('79),
Who always must be firing at the Boche front line.

* * * * *

"Old soldiers never die; they simply fide a-why!"
That's what they used to sing along the roads last spring;
That's what they used to say before the push began;
That's where they are to-day, knocked over to a man.

To Any Dead Officer

Well, how are things in Heaven? I wish you'd say,
   Because I'd like to know that you're all right.
Tell me, have you found everlasting day,
   Or been sucked in by everlasting night?
For when I shut my eyes your face shows plain;
   I hear you make some cheery old remark—
I can rebuild you in my brain,
   Though you've gone out patrolling in the dark.

You hated tours of trenches; you were proud
   Of nothing more than having good years to spend;
Longed to get home and join the careless crowd
   Of chaps who work in peace with Time for friend.
That's all washed out now. You're beyond the wire:
   No earthly chance can send you crawling back;
You've finished with machine-gun fire—
   Knocked over in a hopeless dud-attack.

Somehow I always thought you'd get done in,
   Because you were so desperate keen to live:
You were all out to try and save your skin,
   Well knowing how much the world had got to give.
You joked at shells and talked the usual "shop,"
   Stuck to your dirty job and did it fine:
With "Jesus Christ! when *will* it stop?
   Three years . . . It's hell unless we break their line."

So when they told me you'd been left for dead
   I wouldn't believe them, feeling it must be true.
Next week the bloody Roll of Honour said
   "Wounded and missing"—(That's the thing to do
When lads are left in shell-holes dying slow,
   With nothing but blank sky and wounds that ache,
Moaning for water till they know
   It's night, and then it's not worth while to wake!)

* * * * *

Good-bye, old lad! Remember me to God,
   And tell Him that our Politicians swear
They won't give in till Prussian Rule's been trod
   Under the Heel of England . . . Are you there? . . .

Yes . . . and the War won't end for at least two years;
But we've got stacks of men . . . I'm blind with tears,
   Staring into the dark. Cheero!
I wish they'd killed you in a decent show.

Sick Leave

When I'm asleep, dreaming and lulled and warm,—
They come, the homeless ones, the noiseless dead.
While the dim charging breakers of the storm
Bellow and drone and rumble overhead,
Out of the gloom they gather about my bed.
They whisper to my heart; their thoughts are mine.

"Why are you here with all your watches ended?
From Ypres to Frise we sought you in the Line."
In bitter safety I awake, unfriended;
And while the dawn begins with slashing rain
I think of the Battalion in the mud.
"When are you going out to them again?
Are they not still your brothers through our blood?"

Banishment

I am banished from the patient men who fight.
They smote my heart to pity, built my pride.
Shoulder to aching shoulder, side by side,
They trudged away from life's broad wealds of light.
Their wrongs were mine; and ever in my sight
They went arrayed in honour. But they died,—
Not one by one: and mutinous I cried
To those who sent them out into the night.

The darkness tells how vainly I have striven
To free them from the pit where they must dwell
In outcast gloom convulsed and jagged and riven
By grappling guns. Love drove me to rebel.
Love drives me back to grope with them through hell;
And in their tortured eyes I stand forgiven.

Autumn

October's bellowing anger breaks and cleaves
The bronzed battalions of the stricken wood
In whose lament I hear a voice that grieves
For battle's fruitless harvest, and the feud
Of outraged men. Their lives are like the leaves
Scattered in flocks of ruin, tossed and blown
Along the westering furnace flaring red.
O martyred youth and manhood overthrown,
The burden of your wrongs is on my head.

Repression of War Experience

Now light the candles; one; two; there's a moth;
What silly beggars they are to blunder in
And scorch their wings with glory, liquid flame—
No, no, not that,—it's bad to think of war,
When thoughts you've gagged all day come back to scare you;
And it's been proved that soldiers don't go mad
Unless they lose control of ugly thoughts
That drive them out to jabber among the trees.

Now light your pipe; look, what a steady hand.
Draw a deep breath; stop thinking; count fifteen,
And you're as right as rain . . . Why won't it rain? . . .
I wish there'd be a thunder-storm to-night,
With bucketsful of water to sluice the dark,
And make the roses hang their dripping heads.

Books; what a jolly company they are,
Standing so quiet and patient on their shelves,
Dressed in dim brown, and black, and white, and green
And every kind of colour. Which will you read?
Come on; O *do* read something; they're so wise.
I tell you all the wisdom of the world
Is waiting for you on those shelves; and yet
You sit and gnaw your nails, and let your pipe out,
And listen to the silence: on the ceiling
There's one big, dizzy moth that bumps and flutters;
And in the breathless air outside the house
The garden waits for something that delays.
There must be crowds of ghosts among the trees,—
Not people killed in battle,—they're in France,—
But horrible shapes in shrouds—old men who died
Slow, natural deaths,—old men with ugly souls,
Who wore their bodies out with nasty sins.

                              * * * * *

You're quiet and peaceful, summering safe at home;
You'd never think there was a bloody war on! . . .
O yes, you would . . . why, you can hear the guns.
Hark! Thud, thud, thud,—quite soft . . . they never cease—
Those whispering guns—O Christ, I want to go out
And screech at them to stop—I'm going crazy;
I'm going stark, staring mad because of the guns.

                          Together

Splashing along the boggy woods all day,
And over brambled hedge and holding clay,
I shall not think of him:
But when the watery fields grow brown and dim,
And hounds have lost their fox, and horses tire,
I know that he'll be with me on my way
Home through the darkness to the evening fire.

He's jumped each stile along the glistening lanes;
His hand will be upon the mud-soaked reins;
Hearing the saddle creak,
He'll wonder if the frost will come next week.
I shall forget him in the morning light;
And while we gallop on he will not speak:
But at the stable-door he'll say good-night.

The Hawthorn Tree

Not much to me is yonder lane
   Where I go every day;
But when there's been a shower of rain
   And hedge-birds whistle gay,
I know my lad that's out in France
   With fearsome things to see
Would give his eyes for just one glance
   At our white hawthorn tree.

* * * * *

Not much to me is yonder lane
   Where *he* so longs to tread;
But when there's been a shower of rain
I think I'll never weep again
   Until I've heard he's dead.

Concert Party

(Egyptian Base Camp)

They are gathering round . . .
Out of the twilight; over the grey-blue sand,
Shoals of low-jargoning men drift inward to the sound,—
The jangle and throb of a piano . . . tum-ti-tum . . .
Drawn by a lamp, they come
Out of the glimmering lines of their tents, over the shuffling sand.

O sing us the songs, the songs of our own land,
You warbling ladies in white.
Dimness conceals the hunger in our faces,
This wall of faces risen out of the night,
These eyes that keep their memories of the places
So long beyond their sight.

Jaded and gay, the ladies sing; and the chap in brown
Tilts his grey hat; jaunty and lean and pale,
He rattles the keys . . . some actor-bloke from town . . .

"*God send you home*"; and then "*A long, long trail*";
"*I hear you calling me*"; and "*Dixieland*" . . .
Sing slowly . . . now the chorus . . . one by one
We hear them, drink them; till the concert's done.
Silent, I watch the shadowy mass of soldiers stand.
Silent, they drift away, over the glimmering sand.

                                    KANTARA, *April* 1918.

Night on the Convoy

(ALEXANDRIA-MARSEILLES)

Out in the blustering darkness, on the deck
A gleam of stars looks down. Long blurs of black,
The lean Destroyers, level with our track,
Plunging and stealing, watch the perilous way
Through backward racing seas and caverns of chill spray.

One sentry by the davits, in the gloom
Stands mute; the boat heaves onward through the night.
Shrouded is every chink of cabined light:
And sluiced by floundering waves that hiss and boom
And crash like guns, the troop-ship shudders . . . doom.

Now something at my feet stirs with a sigh;
And slowly growing used to groping dark,
I know that the hurricane-deck, down all its length,
Is heaped and spread with lads in sprawling strength,—
Blanketed soldiers sleeping. In the stark
Danger of life at war, they lie so still,
All prostrate and defenceless, head by head . . .
And I remember Arras, and that hill
Where dumb with pain I stumbled among the dead.

                        * * * * *

We are going home. The troop-ship, in a thrill
Of fiery-chamber'd anguish, throbs and rolls.
We are going home . . . victims . . . three thousand souls.

                                    May 1918.

A Letter Home

(To Robert Graves)

I

Here I'm sitting in the gloom
Of my quiet attic room.
France goes rolling all around,
Fledged with forest May has crowned.
And I puff my pipe, calm-hearted,
Thinking how the fighting started,
Wondering when we'll ever end it,
Back to Hell with Kaiser send it,
Gag the noise, pack up and go,
Clockwork soldiers in a row.
I've got better things to do
Than to waste my time on you.

II

Robert, when I drowse to-night,
Skirting lawns of sleep to chase
Shifting dreams in mazy light,
Somewhere then I'll see your face
Turning back to bid me follow
Where I wag my arms and hollo,
Over hedges hasting after
Crooked smile and baffling laughter,
Running tireless, floating, leaping,
Down your web-hung woods and valleys,
Garden glooms and hornbeam alleys,
Where the glowworm stars are peeping,
Till I find you, quiet as stone
On a hill-top all alone,
Staring outward, gravely pondering
Jumbled leagues of hillock-wandering.

III

You and I have walked together
In the starving winter weather.
We've been glad because we knew
Time's too short and friends are few.
We've been sad because we missed
One whose yellow head was kissed
By the gods, who thought about him

Till they couldn't do without him.
Now he's here again; I've seen
Soldier David dressed in green,
Standing in a wood that swings
To the madrigal he sings.
He's come back, all mirth and glory,
Like the prince in a fairy story.
Winter called him far away;
Blossoms bring him home with May.

IV

Well, I know you'll swear it's true
That you found him decked in blue
Striding up through morning-land
With a cloud on either hand.
Out in Wales, you'll say, he marches
Arm-in-arm with oaks and larches;
Hides all night in hilly nooks,
Laughs at dawn in tumbling brooks.
Yet, it's certain, here he teaches
Outpost-schemes to groups of beeches.
And I'm sure, as here I stand,
That he shines through every land,
That he sings in every place
Where we're thinking of his face.

V

Robert, there's a war in France;
Everywhere men bang and blunder,
Sweat and swear and worship Chance,
Creep and blink through cannon thunder.
Rifles crack and bullets flick,
Sing and hum like hornet-swarms.
Bones are smashed and buried quick.
Yet, through stunning battle storms.
All the while I watch the spark
Lit to guide me; for I know
Dreams will triumph, though the dark
Scowls above me where I go.
You can hear me; *you* can mingle
Radiant folly with my jingle,
War's a joke for me and you
While we know such dreams are true!

Reconciliation

When you are standing at your hero's grave,
Or near some homeless village where he died,
Remember, through your heart's rekindling pride,
The German soldiers who were loyal and brave.

Men fought like brutes; and hideous things were done:
And you have nourished hatred, harsh and blind.
But in that Golgotha perhaps you'll find
The mothers of the men who killed your son.

November 1918.

Memorial Tablet

(GREAT WAR)

Squire nagged and bullied till I went to fight
(Under Lord Derby's scheme). I died in hell—
(They called it Passchendaele); my wound was slight,
And I was hobbling back, and then a shell
Burst slick upon the duck-boards; so I fell
Into the bottomless mud, and lost the light.

In sermon-time, while Squire is in his pew,
He gives my gilded name a thoughtful stare;
For though low down upon the list, I'm there:
"In proud and glorious memory"—that's my due.
Two bleeding years I fought in France for Squire;
I suffered anguish that he's never guessed;
Once I came home on leave; and then went west.
What greater glory could a man desire?

The Death-Bed

He drowsed and was aware of silence heaped
Round him, unshaken as the steadfast walls;
Aqueous like floating rays of amber light,
Soaring and quivering in the wings of sleep,—
Silence and safety; and his mortal shore
Lipped by the inward, moonless waves of death.

Some one was holding water to his mouth.
He swallowed, unresisting; moaned and dropped
Through crimson gloom to darkness; and forgot
The opiate throb and ache that was his wound.
Water—calm, sliding green above the weir;

Water—a sky-lit alley for his boat,
Bird-voiced, and bordered with reflected flowers
And shaken hues of summer: drifting down,
He dipped contented oars, and sighed, and slept.

Night, with a gust of wind, was in the ward,
Blowing the curtain to a glimmering curve.
Night. He was blind; he could not see the stars
Glinting among the wraiths of wandering cloud;
Queer blots of colour, purple, scarlet, green,
Flickered and faded in his drowning eyes.

Rain; he could hear it rustling through the dark;
Fragrance and passionless music woven as one;
Warm rain on drooping roses; pattering showers
That soak the woods; not the harsh rain that sweeps
Behind the thunder, but a trickling peace
Gently and slowly washing life away.

* * * * *

He stirred, shifting his body; then the pain
Leaped like a prowling beast, and gripped and tore
His groping dreams with grinding claws and fangs.
But some one was beside him; soon he lay
Shuddering because that evil thing had passed.
And Death, who'd stepped toward him, paused and stared.

Light many lamps and gather round his bed.
Lend him your eyes, warm blood, and will to live.
Speak to him; rouse him; you may save him yet.
He's young; he hated war; how should he die
When cruel old campaigners win safe through?

But Death replied: "I choose him." So he went,
And there was silence in the summer night;
Silence and safety; and the veils of sleep.
Then, far away, the thudding of the guns.

Aftermath

Have you forgotten yet? . . .
For the world's events have rumbled on since those gagged days,
Like traffic checked awhile at the crossing of city ways:
And the haunted gap in your mind has filled with thoughts that flow
Like clouds in the lit heavens of life; and you're a man reprieved to go,
Taking your peaceful share of Time, with joy to spare.
But the past is just the same,—and War's a bloody game. . . .

Have you forgotten yet? . . .
Look down, and swear by the slain of the War that you'll never forget.

Do you remember the dark months you held the sector at Mametz,—
The nights you watched and wired and dug and piled sandbags on parapets?
Do you remember the rats; and the stench
Of corpses rotting in front of the front-line trench,—
And dawn coming, dirty-white, and chill with a hopeless rain?
Do you ever stop and ask, "Is it all going to happen again?"

Do you remember that hour of din before the attack,—
And the anger, the blind compassion that seized and shook you then
As you peered at the doomed and haggard faces of your men?
Do you remember the stretcher-cases lurching back
With dying eyes and lolling heads,—those ashen-grey
Masks of the lads who once were keen and kind and gay?

Have you forgotten yet? . . .
Look up, and swear by the green of the Spring that you'll never forget.

Song-Books of the War

In fifty years, when peace outshines
Remembrance of the battle lines,
Adventurous lads will sigh and cast
Proud looks upon the plundered past.
On summer morn or winter's night,
Their hearts will kindle for the fight,
Reading a snatch of soldier-song,
Savage and jaunty, fierce and strong;
And through the angry marching rhymes
Of blind regret and haggard mirth,
They'll envy us the dazzling times
When sacrifice absolved our earth.

Some ancient man with silver locks
Will lift his weary face to say:
"War was a fiend who stopped our clocks
Although we met him grim and gay."
And then he'll speak of Haig's last drive,
Marvelling that any came alive
Out of the shambles that men built
And smashed, to cleanse the world of guilt.
But the boys, with grin and sidelong glance,
Will think, "Poor grandad's day is done."
And dream of lads who fought in France
And lived in time to share the fun.

Everyone Sang

Everyone suddenly burst out singing;
And I was filled with such delight
As prisoned birds must find in freedom
Winging wildly across the white
Orchards and dark green fields; on; on; and out of sight.

Everyone's voice was suddenly lifted,
And beauty came like the setting sun.
My heart was shaken with tears and horror
Drifted away . . . O but every one
Was a bird; and the song was wordless; the singing will never be done.

April 1919.

THE POEMS OF IVOR GURNEY

Severn and Somme

To Certain Comrades

(E. S. AND J. H.)

Living we loved you, yet withheld our praises
Before your faces;

And though we had your spirits high in honour,
After the English manner

We said no word. Yet, as such comrades would,
You understood.

Such friendship is not touched by Death's disaster,
But stands the faster;

And all the shocks and trials of time cannot
Shake it one jot.

Beside the fire at night some far December,
We shall remember

And tell men, unbegotten as yet, the story
Of your sad glory—

Of your plain strength, your truth of heart, your splendid
Coolness, all ended!

All ended, . . . yet the aching hearts of lovers
Joy overcovers,

Glad in their sorrow; hoping that if they must
Come to the dust,

An ending such as yours may be their portion,
And great good fortune—

That if we may not live to serve in peace
England, watching increase—

Then death with you, honoured, and swift, and high;
And so—not die.

IN TRENCHES, *July* 1916.

The Fire Kindled

God, that I might see
    Framilode once again!
Redmarley, all renewed,
    Clear shining after rain.

And Cranham, Cranham trees,
    And blaze of Autumn hues.
Portway under the moon,
    Silvered with freezing dews.

May Hill that Gloster dwellers
    'Gainst every sunset see;
And the wide Severn river
    Homing again to the sea.

The star of afterglow,
    Venus, on western hills;
Dymock in spring: O spring
    Of home! O daffodils!

And Malvern's matchless huge
    Bastions of ancient fires—
These will not let me rest,
    So hot my heart desires....

Here we go sore of shoulder,
    Sore of foot, by quiet streams;
But these are not my rivers. . . .
    And these are useless dreams.

To the Poet Before Battle

Now, youth, the hour of thy dread passion comes:
Thy lovely things must all be laid away;
And thou, as others, must face the riven day
Unstirred by rattle of the rolling drums,
Or bugles' strident cry. When mere noise numbs
The sense of being, the fear-sick soul doth sway,
Remember thy great craft's honour, that they may say
Nothing in shame of poets. Then the crumbs
Of praise the little versemen joyed to take
Shall be forgotten: then they must know we are,
For all our skill in words, equal in might
And strong of mettle as those we honoured; make
The name of poet terrible in just war,
And like a crown of honour upon the fight.

Maisemore

O when we swung through Maisemore,
   The Maisemore people cheered,
And women ran from farmyards,
   And men from ricks, afeared

To lose the sight of soldiers
   Who would, 'fore Christmas Day,
Blow Kaiser William's Army
   Like mist of breath away!

The war it was but young then!
   And we were young, unknowing
The path we were to tread,
   The way the path was going.

And not a man of all of us,
   Marching across the bridge,
Had thought how Home would linger
   In our hearts, as Maisemore Ridge.

When the darkness downward hovers
   Making trees like German shadows,
How our souls fly homing, homing
   Times and times to Maisemore meadows,

By Aubers ridge that Maisemore men
  Have died in vain to hold. . . .
The burning thought but once desires
  Maisemore in morning gold!

O when we marched through Maisemore
  Past many a creaking cart,
We little thought we had in us
  Love so hot at heart.

Afterwards

Those dreadful evidences of Man's ill-doing
The kindly Mother of all shall soon hide deep,
Covering with tender fingers her children asleep,
Till Time's slow cycle turns them to renewing
In other forms their beauty—no grief, no rueing
Irrevocable woe. They'll lie, they'll steep
Their hearts in peace unfathomed, till they leap
Quick to the light of the sun, as flowers strewing,
Maybe, their own friends' paths. And that's not all.
When men who knew them walk old ways alone,
The paths they loved together, at even-fall,
The troubled heart shall know a presence near,
Friendly, familiar, and the old grief gone,
The new keen joy shall make all darkness clear.

Carol

Winter now has bared the trees,
  Killed with tiny swords the jolly
Leafage that mid-summer sees,
  But left the ivy and the holly.
Hold them high
And make delight
For Christë's joy that's born to-night.

All green things but these have hid
  Their heads, or died in melancholy,
Winter's spite them all has rid
  Save only ivy and brave holly.
Give them place
In all men's sight
For Christë's grace that's born to-night.

Baby eyes are pleased to see
   Bright red berries and children jolly,
So shout and dance and sing with glee,
   And honour ivy and prickly holly.
      Honour courage
      And make delight
For Christë's sake that's born to-night.

Christus natus hodie!
   Drink deep of joy on Christmas Day,
Join hands and sing a roundelay,
   For this is Christ's and children's day,
      Christus natus hodie!
        Hodie!

Strange Service

Little did I dream, England, that you bore me
Under the Cotswold hills beside the water meadows,
To do you dreadful service, here, beyond your borders
And your enfolding seas.

I was a dreamer ever, and bound to your dear service,
Meditating deep, I thought on your secret beauty,
As through a child's face one may see the clear spirit
Miraculously shining.

Your hills not only hills, but friends of mine and kindly,
Your tiny knolls and orchards hidden beside the river
Muddy and strongly-flowing, with shy and tiny streamlets
Safe in its bosom.

Now these are memories only, and your skies and rushy sky-pools
Fragile mirrors easily broken by moving airs. . . .
In my deep heart for ever goes on your daily being,
And uses consecrate.

Think on me too, O Mother, who wrest my soul to serve you
In strange and fearful ways beyond your encircling waters;
None but you can know my heart, its tears and sacrifice;
None, but you, repay.

Serenity

Nor steel nor flame has any power on me,
Save that its malice work the Almighty Will,
Nor steel nor flame has any power on me;
Through tempests of hell-fire I must go free
And unafraid; so I remember still
Nor steel nor flame has any power on me,
Save that its malice work the Almighty Will.

The Signaller's Vision

One rainy winter dusk
   Mending a parted cable,
Sudden I saw so clear
   Home and the tea-table.

So clear it was, so sweet,
   I did not start, but drew
The breath of deep content
   Some minutes ere I knew

My Mother's face that's soother
   Than autumn half-lights kind,
My softly smiling sisters
   Who keep me still in mind,

Were but a dream, a vision—
   That faded. And I knew
The smell of trench, trench-feeling—
   And turned to work anew.

The Mother

We scar the earth with dreadful engin'ry;
She takes us to her bosom at the last;
Hiding our hate with love, who cannot see
Of any child the faults; and holds us fast.
We'll wait in quiet till our passion's past.

To England—A Note

I watched the boys of England where they went
Through mud and water to do appointed things.
See one a stake, and one wire-netting brings,
And one comes slowly under a burden bent
Of ammunition. Though the strength be spent

They "carry on" under the shadowing wings
Of Death the ever-present. And hark, one sings
Although no joy from the grey skies be lent.

Are these the heroes—these? have kept from you
The power of primal savagery so long?
Shall break the devil's legions? These they are
Who do in silence what they might boast to do;
In the height of battle tell the world in song
How they do hate and fear the face of War.

Bach and the Sentry

Watching the dark my spirit rose in flood
    On that most dearest Prelude of my delight.
The low-lying mist lifted its hood,
    The October stars showed nobly in clear night.

When I return, and to real music-making,
    And play that Prelude, how will it happen then?
Shall I feel as I felt, a sentry hardly waking,
    With a dull sense of No Man's Land again?

Letters

"Mail's up!" The vast of night is over,
And love of friends fills all one's mind.
(His wife, his sister, or his lover.)
Mail's up, the vast of night is over,
The grey-faced heaven joy does cover
With love, and God once more seems kind.
"Mail's up!" the vast of night is over,
And love of friends fills all one's mind.

Strafe

The "crumps" are falling twenty to the minute.
We crouch, and wait the end of it—or us.
Just behind the trench, before, and in it,
The "crumps" are falling twenty to the minute;
(O Framilode! O Maisemore's laughing linnet!)
Here comes a monster like a motor-bus.
The "crumps" are falling twenty to the minute:
We crouch and wait the end of it—or us.

Acquiescence

Since I can neither alter my destiny
By one hair's breadth from its appointed course;
Since bribes nor prayers nor any earthly force
May from its pathway move a life not free—
I must gather together the whole strength of me.
My senses make my willing servitors;
Cherish and feed the better, starve the worse;
Turn all my pride to proud humility.
Meeting the daily shocks and frozen, stony,
Cynical face of doubt with smiles and joy—
As a battle with autumn winds delights a boy,
Before the smut of the world and the lust of money,
Power, and fame, can yet his youth destroy;
Ere he has scorned his Father's patrimony.

The Strong Thing

I have seen Death and the faces of men in fear
    Of Death, and shattered, terribly ruined flesh,
Appalled; but through the horror, coloured and clear
    The love of my county, Gloster, rises afresh.

And on the Day of Days, the Judgment Day,
    The Word of Doom awaiting breathless and still,
I'll marvel how sweet's the air down Framilode way,
    And take my sentence on sheer-down Crickley Hill.

Scots

The boys who laughed and jested with me but yesterday,
So fit for kings to speak to, so blithe and proud and gay ...
Are now but thoughts of blind pain, and best hid away....
(Over the top this morning at the dawn's first grey.)

O, if we catch the Kaiser his dirty hide to flay,
We'll hang him on a tall tree his pride to allay.
That will not bring the boys again to mountain and brac....
(Over the top this morning at the dawn's first grey.)

To think—earth's best and dearest turned to red broken clay
By one devil's second! What words can we say?
Or what gift has God their mothers' anguish to repay?...
(Over the top this morning at the first flush of day.)

To An Unknown Lady

You that were once so sweet, are sweeter now
That an even leaden greyness clouds my days;
A pain it is to think on your sweet ways,
Your careless-tender speaking, tender and low.
When the hills enclosed us, hid in happy valleys,
Greeting a thousand times the things most dear,
We wasted thoughts of love in laughter clear,
And told our passion out in mirthful sallies.
But in me now a burning impulse rages
To praise our love in words like flaming gold,
Molten and live for ever; not fit for cold
And coward like-to-passions Time assuages.
Nor do I fear you are lovely only in dreams,
Being as the sky reflected in clear streams.

Song and Pain

Out of my sorrow have I made these songs,
        Out of my sorrow;
Though somewhat of the making's eager pain
        From Joy did borrow.

Some day, I trust, God's purpose of Pain for me
        Shall be complete,
And then—to enter in the House of Joy. . . .
        Prepare, my feet.

Purple and Black

The death of princes is
    Honoured most greatly,
Proud kings put purple on
    In manner stately.

Though they have lived such life
    As God offends,
Gone fearful down to death,
    Sick, without friends.

And in the temple dim,
    Trumpets of gold
Proclaim their glory; so
    Their story is told.

In sentimental hymns
   Weeping her dolour,
The mother of heroes wears
   Vile black—Death's colour,

Who should walk proudly with
   The noblest one
Of all that purple throng—
   "This was my son."

West Country

Spring comes soon to Maisemore
   And spring comes sweet,
With bird-songs and blue skies,
   On gay dancing feet;
But she is such a shy lady
   I fear we'll never meet.

Yet some day round a corner
   Where the hedge foams white,
I'll find Spring sleeping
   In the young-crescent night,
And seize her and make her
   Yield all her delight.

But yon's a glad story
   That's yet to be told.
Here's grey winter's bareness
   And no-shadowed cold.
O Spring, with your music,
   Your blue, green, and gold,
Come shame his hard wisdom
   With laughter and gold!

Firelight

Silent, bathed in firelight, in dusky light and gloom
The boys squeeze together in the smoky dirty room,
Crowded round the fireplace, a thing of bricks and tin,
They watch the shifting embers till the good dreams enter in,

That fill the low hovel with blossoms fresh with dew,
And blue sky and white clouds that sail the clear air through.
They talk of daffodillies and the bluebells' skiey bed,
Till silence thrills and murmurs at the things they have said.

And yet, they have no skill of words, whose eyes glow so deep,
They wait for night and silence and the strange power of sleep,
To lift them and drift them like sea-birds over the sea
Where some day I shall walk again, and they walk with me.

The Estaminet

The crowd of us were drinking
    One night at Riez Bailleul,
The glasses were a-clinking,
    The estaminet was full;

And loud with song and story
    And blue with tales and smoke,—
We spoke no word of glory,
    Nor mentioned "foreign yoke."

But yarns of girls in Blighty;
    Vain, jolly, ugly, fair,
Standoffish, foolish, flighty—
    And O! that we were there!

Where never thuds a "Minnie,"
    But Minnie smiles at you
A-meeting in the spinney,
    With kisses not a few.

And of an inn that Johnson
    Does keep; the "Rising Sun."
His friends him call Jack Johnson,
    He's Gloster's only one.

And talk of poachers' habits
    (But girls ever and again)
Of killing weasels, rabbits,
    Stoats, pheasants, never men,

Although we knew to-morrow
    Must take us to the line,
In beer hid thought and sorrow,
    In ruddy and white wine.

When all had finished drinking,
    Though still was clear each head,
We said no word—went slinking
    Straight homeward (?), into bed (?).

O never lads were merrier
    Nor straighter nor more fine,
Though we were only "Terrier"
    And only, "Second Line."

O I may get to Blighty,
    Or hell, without a sign
Of all the love that filled me,
    Leave dumb the love that filled me,
The flood of love that filled me
    For these dear comrades of mine.

Song

Only the wanderer
    Knows England's graces,
Or can anew see clear
    Familiar faces.

And who loves joy as he
    That dwells in shadows?
Do not forget me quite,
    O Severn meadows.

Ballad of the Three Spectres

As I went up by Ovillers
    In mud and water cold to the knee,
There went three jeering, fleering spectres,
    That walked abreast and talked of me.

The first said, "Here's a right brave soldier
    That walks the dark unfearingly;
Soon he'll come back on a fine stretcher,
    And laughing for a nice Blighty."

The second, "Read his face, old comrade,
    No kind of lucky chance I see;
One day he'll freeze in mud to the marrow,
    Then look his last on Picardie."

Though bitter the word of these first twain
    Curses the third spat venomously;
"He'll stay untouched till the war's last dawning
    Then live one hour of agony."

Liars the first two were. Behold me
   At sloping arms by one—two—three;
Waiting the time I shall discover
   Whether the third spake verity.

Communion

Beauty lies so deep
   On all the fields,
Nothing for the eyes
   But blessing yields.

Tall elms, greedy of light,
   Stand tip-toe. See
The last light linger in
   Their tracery.

The guns are dumb, are still
   All evil noises.
The singing heart in peace
   Softly rejoices,

Only unsatisfied
   With Beauty's hunger
And sacramental thirst—
   Nothing of anger.

Mist wraiths haunt the path
   As daylight lessens,
The stars grow clearer, and
   My dead friend's presence.

Time and the Soldier

How slow you move, old Time;
   Walk a bit faster!
Old fool, I'm not your slave. . . .
   Beauty's my master!

You hold me for a space. . . .
   What are you, Time?
A ghost, a thing of thought,
   An easy rhyme.

Some day I shall again,
   For all your scheming,
See Severn valley clouds
   Like banners streaming.

And walk in Cranham lanes,
   By Maisemore go. . . .
But, fool, decrepit Fool,
   You are SO SLOW!!!

Influences

When woods of home grow dark,
   I grow dark too.
Images of strange power
Fill me and thrill me that hour,
   Sombre of hue.

The woods of Dunsinane
   I walk, and know
What storms did shake Macbeth,
That brought on Duncan's death,
   And his own woe.

Strange whispers chill the blood
   Of evil breath;
Such rumours as did stir
Witch and foul sorcerer
   On the lone heath.

No power have these on me;
   I know too well
Their weakness to condemn.
Spring will exorcise them
   With one bluebell.

After-Glow

[*To* F. W. HARVEY]

Out of the smoke and dust of the little room
With tea-talk loud and laughter of happy boys,
I passed into the dusk. Suddenly the noise
Ceased with a shock, left me alone in the gloom,
To wonder at the miracle hanging high
Tangled in twigs, the silver crescent clear.—
Time passed from mind. Time died; and then we were

Once more at home together, you and I.

The elms with arms of love wrapped us in shade
Who watched the ecstatic West with one desire,
One soul uprapt; and still another fire
Consumed us, and our joy yet greater made:
That Bach should sing for us, mix us in one
The joy of firelight and the sunken sun.

Hail and Farewell

The destined bullet wounded him,
    They brought him down to die,
Far-off a bugle sounded him
    "Retreat," Good-bye.

Strange, that from ways so hated,
    And tyranny so hard
Should come this strangely fated
    And farewell word.

He thought, "Some Old Sweat might
    Have thrilled at heart to hear,
Gone down into the night
    Too proud to fear!

But I—the fool at arms,
    Musician, poet to boot,
Who hail release; what charms
    In this salute?"

He smiled—"The latest jest
    That time on me shall play."
And watched the dying west,
    Went out with the day.

Praise

O friends of mine, if men mock at my name,
Say "Children loved him."
Since by that word you will have far removed him
From any bitter shame.

Winter Beauty

I cannot live with Beauty out of mind;
   I seek her and desire her all the day,
Being the chiefest treasure man may find,
   And word most sweet his eager lips can say.
She is as strong on me as though I wandered
   In Severn meadows some blue riotous day.

But since the trees have long since lost their green,
   And I, an exile, can but dream of things
Grown magic in the mind, I watch the sheen
   Of frost and hear the song Orion sings,
And hear the star-born passion of Beethoven;
   Man's consolations sung on the quivering strings.

Beauty of song remembered, sunset glories,
   Mix in my mind, till I not care nor know
Whether the stars do move me, golden stories,
   Or ruddy Cotswold in the sunset glow.
I am uprapt, and not my own, immortal, . . .
   In winds of Beauty swinging to and fro.

Beauty immortal, not to be hid, desire
   Of all men, each in his fashion, give me the strong
Thirst past satisfaction for thee, and fire
   Not to be quenched. . . . O lift me, bear me along,
Touch me, make me worthy that men may seek me
   For Beauty, Mistress Immortal, Healer of Wrong.

Song of Pain and Beauty

[*To* M. M. S.]

O may these days of pain,
   These wasted-seeming days,
Somewhere reflower again
   With scent and savour of praise.
Draw out of memory all bitterness
   Of night with Thy sun's rays.

And strengthen Thou in me
   The love of men here found,
And eager charity,
   That, out of difficult ground,
Spring like flowers in barren deserts, or
   Like light, or a lovely sound.

A simpler heart than mine
  Might have seen beauty clear
Where I could see no sign
  Of Thee, but only fear.
Strengthen me, make me to see Thy beauty always
  In every happening here.

IN TRENCHES, *March 1917.*

Spring. Rouen, May 1917

I am dumb, I am dumb!
And here's a Norman orchard and here's Spring
Goading the sullen words that will not come.
Romance, beating his distant magical drum,
Calls to a soldier bearing alien arms,
"Throw off your yoke and hear my darlings sing,
Blackbirds" (by red-roofed farms)
"More drunk than any poet with May's delight,
Green alive to the eye, and pink and white."

Joy's there, but not for me;
And song, but shall I sing
That live as in a dream of some bad night,
Whose memories are of such ecstasy
And height of passionate joy, that pain alone
Is born of beauty in cloud and flower and tree;
Yes, and the great Cathedral's towering stone.

To me these are but shadows
Of orchards and old meadows
Trodden before the dawn,
Trodden after the dusk. . . .
All loveliness of France is as a husk,
The inner living spirit of beauty gone,
To that familiar beauty now withdrawn
From exiles hungering ever for the sight
Of her day-face;
England's;
Or in some orchard space
Breathless to drink peace from her calm night.

How shall I sing, since she sings not to me
Songs any more?
High rule she holds for ever on the sea
That's hers, but dreams too might guard the shore
Of France, that's French and set apart for ever.
A Spirit of Love our link of song does sever.

Had it been hate
(The weakest of all sworn enemies of Love)
We should have broken through or passed above
Its foolish barriers;
Here we must bow as to established Fate,
And reverently; for, comrades and high peers,
Sisters in blood,
Our mothers brook no rival in their state
Of motherhood.

But not for ever shall our travail last,
And not for ever we
Be held by iron Duty over sea.
The image of evil shall be overcast,
And all his willing slaves and priests of evil
Scattered like dust, shall lie upon the plain;
That image, ground to dust utterly level
With unregarded weeds and all as vain.
The oppressed shall lift their hearts up once again,
And we return. . . .
Not to scarred lands and homes laid in the dust,
Not with hard hearts to sights that sear and burn,
But with assured longing and certain trust,
To England's royal grace and dignity,
To England's changing skies, rich greenery,
High strength controlled, queenly serenity,
Inviolate kept by her confederate sea
And hearts resolved to every sacrifice.
We shall come home,
We shall come home again,
Living and dead, one huge victorious host—
The dead that would not leave their comrades till
The last steep were topped of the difficult hill,
The last farthing paid of the Great Cost,
The last thrill suffered of the Great Pain.
Living and dead, we shall come home at last
To her sweet breast,
England's; by one touch be paid in full
For all things grey and long and terrible
Of that dread night which seemed eternity.

O Mother, shall thy kisses not restore
Body and life-sick soul? Yes, and set free
Songs and great floods of lovelier melody
Than thou didst give
When we those days of half-awake did live.
And joy must surely flower again more fair
To us, who dwelt in shadows and foul air.

We'll breathe and drink in song.

Spring shall blot out all traces of old care;
Her clouds of green and waves of gold among
We shall grow free of heart, and great, and young—
Be made anew in that Great Resurrection,
Perfect as is the violet's perfection.
Perfect as she
Who sanctifies our memory with sorrow,
Hugs, as a mother hugs, the thoughts that harrow,
Watching for dawn, hungering for the morrow
Lone oversea. . . .

I am dumb now, dumb,
But in that time what music shall not come?
Mother of Beauty, Mistress of the Sea.

June—To—Come

When the sun's fire and gold
    Sets the bee humming,
I will not write to tell
    Him that I'm coming,

But ride out unawares
    On that old road,
Of Minsterworth, of Peace,
    Of Framilode,

And walk, not looked for, in
    That cool, dark passage.
Never a single word;
    Myself my message.

And then; well . . . O we'll drift
    And stand and gaze,
And wonder how we could
    In those Bad Days

Live without Minsterworth;
    Or western air
Fanning the hot cheek,
    Stirring the hair;

In land where hate of men
    God's love did cover;
This land. . . . And here's my dream
    Irrevocably over.

"Hark, Hark, The Lark"

Hark, hark, the lark to heaven's gate uprisen,
   Pours out his joy . . .
I think of you, shut in some distant prison,
   O Boy, poor Boy;

Your heart grown sick with hope deferred and shadows
   Of prison ways;
Not daring to snatch a thought of Severn meadows,
   Or old blue-days.

Song at Morning

Praise for the day's magnificent uprising!
Praise for the cool
Air and the blue new-old ever-surprising
Face of the sky, and mirrored blue of the pool.
Only the fool, bat-witted, owl-eyed fool
Can hold a deaf ear while life begins
The actual opening of a myriad stories. . . .
Blindness, ingratitude, the foolishest sins!
Now if this day blot out my chief desires,
And leave me maimed and blind and full of hot
Surges of insurrection, evil fires,
Memories of joys that seem better forgot;
Quiet me then.
Thy Will is binding on the nearest flower
As on the farthest star; and what shall put me
Out of Thy power, or from Thy guidance far,
Though I in hell of my self-will would shut me?
But if Thy Will be joy for me to-day,
Give me clear eyes, a heart open to feel
Thy influence, Thy kindness: O unseal
The shut, the hidden places in me, reveal
Those things most precious secretly hidden away
From all save children and the simply wise.
Give me clear eyes!
And strength to know, whatever may befall,
The eternal presence of great mysteries,
Glorifying Thee for all.

Trees

("You cannot think how ghastly these battle-fields look under a grey sky.
Torn trees are the most terrible things I have ever seen. Absolute blight and
curse is on the face of everything.")

The dead land oppressed me;
    I turned my thoughts away,
And went where hill and meadow
    Are shadowless and gay.

Where Coopers stands by Cranham,
    Where the hill-gashes white
Show golden in the sunshine,
    Our sunshine—God's delight.

Beauty my feet stayed at last
    Where green was most cool,
Trees worthy of all worship
    I worshipped . . . then, O fool,

Let my thoughts slide unwitting
    To other, dreadful trees, . . .
And found me standing, staring
    Sick of heart—at these!

Requiem

Pour out your light, O stars, and do not hold
    Your loveliest shining from earth's outworn shell—
Pure and cold your radiance, pure and cold
    My dead friend's face as well.

Requiem

Nor grief nor tears should wrong the silent dead
    Save England's, for her children fallen so far
From her eager care; though by God's justice led
    And fallen in such a war.

Requiem

Pour out your bounty, moon of radiant shining
    On all this shattered flesh, these quiet forms;
For these were slain, so strangely still reclining,
    In the noblest cause was ever waged with arms.

Sonnets 1917

[*To* the Memory of Rupert Brooke]

1. FOR ENGLAND

Though heaven be packed with joy-bewildering
Pleasures of soul and heart and mind, yet who
Would willingly let slip, freely let go
Earth's mortal loveliness; go wandering
Where never the late bird is heard to sing,
Nor full-sailed cloud-galleons wander slow;
No pathways in the woods; no afterglow,
When the air's fire and magic with sense of spring?

So the dark horror clouds us, and the dread
Of the unknown. . . . But if it must be, then
What better passing than to go out like men
For England, giving all in one white glow?
Whose bodies shall lie in earth as on a bed,
And as the Will directs our spirits may go

2. PAIN

Pain, pain continual; pain unending;
Hard even to the roughest, but to those
Hungry for beauty.... Not the wisest knows,
Nor most pitiful-hearted, what the wending
Of one hour's way meant. Grey monotony lending
Weight to the grey skies, grey mud where goes
An army of grey bedrenched scarecrows in rows
Careless at last of cruellest Fate-sending.
Seeing the pitiful eyes of men foredone,
Or horses shot, too tired merely to stir,
Dying in shell-holes both, slain by the mud.
Men broken, shrieking even to hear a gun.—
Till pain grinds down, or lethargy numbs her,
The amazed heart cries angrily out on God.

3. SERVITUDE

If it were not for England, who would bear
This heavy servitude one moment more?
To keep a brothel, sweep and wash the floor
Of filthiest hovels were noble to compare
With this brass-cleaning life. Now here, now there
Harried in foolishness, scanned curiously o'er

By fools made brazen by conceit, and store
Of antique witticisms thin and bare.

Only the love of comrades sweetens all,
Whose laughing spirit will not be outdone.
As night-watching men wait for the sun
To hearten them, so wait I on such boys
As neither brass nor Hell-fire may appal,
Nor guns, nor sergeant-major's bluster and noise.

4. HOME-SICKNESS

When we go wandering the wide air's blue spaces,
Bare, unhappy, exiled souls of men;
How will our thoughts over and over again
Return to Earth's familiar lovely places,
Where light with shadow ever interlaces—
No blanks of blue, nor ways beyond man's ken—
Where birds are, and flowers, as violet, and wren,
Blackbird, bluebell, hedge-sparrow, tiny daisies.

O tiny things, but very stuff of soul
To us . . . so frail. . . . Remember what we are;
Set us not on some strange outlandish star,
But one caring for Love. Give us a Home.
There we may wait while the long ages roll
Content, unfrightened by vast Time-to-come.

5. ENGLAND THE MOTHER

We have done our utmost, England, terrible
And dear taskmistress, darling Mother and stern.
The unnoticed nations praise us, but we turn
Firstly, only to thee—"Have we done well?
Say, are you pleased?"—and watch your eyes that tell
To us all secrets, eyes sea-deep that burn
With love so long denied; with tears discern
The scars and haggard look of all that hell.

Thy love, thy love shall cherish, make us whole,
Whereto the power of Death's destruction is weak.
Death impotent, by boys bemocked at, who
Will leave unblotted in the soldier-soul
Gold of the daffodil, the sunset streak,
The innocence and joy of England's blue.

War's Embers and Other Verses

Dedication: To M. M. S.

O, if my wishes were my power,
You should be praised as were most fit,
Whose kindness cannot help but flower.

But since the fates have ordered it
Otherwise, then ere the hour
Of darkness deaden all my wit

I'll write: how all my art was poor,
My mind too thought-packed to acquit
My debt . . . And only, "Thanks once more."

The Volunteer

(To A. L. B.)

I would test God's purposes:
  I will go up and see
What fate He'll give, what destiny
  His hand holds for me.

For God is very secret,
  Slow-smiles, but does not say
A word that will foreshadow
  Shape of the coming day.

Curious am I, curious . . .
  And since He will not tell
I'll prove Him, go up against
  The naked mouth of Hell.

And what hereafter—Heaven?
  Or Blighty? O if it were . . .
Mere agony, mere pain the price
  Of the returning there.

Or—nothing! Days in mud
  And slush, then other days . . .
Aie me! "Are they not all
  The seas of God"; God's Ways?

The Farm

(TO MRS. HARVEY AND THOSE OTHERS)

A creeper-covered house, an orchard near;
A farmyard with tall ricks upstanding clear
In golden sunlight of a late September.——
How little of a whole world to remember!
How slight a thing to keep a spirit free!
Within the house were books,
A piano, dear to me,
And round the house the rooks
Haunted each tall elm tree;
Each sunset crying, calling, clamouring aloud.

And friends lived there of whom the house was proud,
Sheltering with content from wind and storm,
Them loving gathered at the hearthside warm,
(O friendly, happy crowd!)
Caress of firelight gave them, touching hair
And cheeks and hands with sombre gleams of love,
(When day died out behind the lovely bare
Network of twigs, orchard and elms apart;
When rooks lay still in round dark nests above,
And Peace like cool dew comforted the heart.)

The house all strangers welcomed, but as strangers kept
For ever them apart
From its deep heart,
That hidden sanctuary of love close guarded;
Having too great a honey-heap uphoarded
Of children's play, men's work, lightly to let
Strangers therein;
Who knew its stubborn pride, and loved the more
The place from webbed slate roof to cellar floor—
Hens clucking, ducks, all casual farmyard din.
How empty the place seemed when Duty called
To harder service its three sons than tending
Brown fruitful good earth there! But all's God's sending.
Above the low barn where the oxen were stalled
The old house watched for weeks the road, to see
Nothing but common traffic; nothing its own.
It had grown to them so used, so long had known
Their presences; sheltered and shared sorrow and glee,
No wonder it felt desolate and left alone ...
That must remember, nothing at all forget.
My mind (how often!) turned and returned to it,

When in queer holes of chance, bedraggled, wet,
Lousy I lay; to think how by Severn-side
A house of steadfastness and quiet pride
Kept faith to friends (when hope of mine had died
Almost to ash). And never twilight came
With mystery and peace and points of flame—
Save it must bring sounds of my Severn flowing
Steadily seawards, orange windows glowing
Bright in the dusk, and many a well-known name.

Omens

(To E. H.)

Black rooks about the trees
   Are circling slow;
Tall elms that can no ease
   Nor comfort know,
Since that the Autumn wind
Batters them before, behind,
A bitter breeze unkind.

They call like tongues of dread
   Prophesying woe,
Rooks on the sunset red,
   Not heeding how
Their clamouring brings near
To a woman the old fear
For her far soldier dear.

That harsh and idle crying
   Of mere annoy
Tells her how men are dying,
   And how her boy
May lie, his racked thought turning
To the home fire on the hearth burning,
The last agony be learning.

Eternal Treasure

(To H. N. H.)

Why think on Beauty as for ever lost
When fire and steel have worked their evil will,
Since Beauty lasts beyond decaying dust,
And in the after-dark is lovely still?
We are no phantoms; Body is but the case
Of an immortal Flame that does not perish,

Can the all-withering power of Time outface,
Since God Himself with love that flame does cherish.
Take comfort then, and dare the dangerous thing,
Death flouting with his impotence of wrath;
For Beauty arms us 'gainst his envious sting,
Safes us in any the most perilous path.
Come then, O brothers, greet what may befall
With Joy, for Beauty's Maker ordereth all.

Fire in the Dusk

When your white hands have lost their fairy power,
Like dimpling water flash and charm no more,
Quick pride of grace is still, closed your bright eyes—
I still must think, under those Northern skies,
Some influence shall remain of all that sweet;
Some flower of courage braving Easter sleet;
Colour to stir tears in tenderest skies;
Music of light. Your Autumn beeches shall
Set passion blazing in a heart until
Colour you gave be fashioned in formal line
On line; another's beauty prove divine,
And all your wandering grace shall not be lost
To earth, being too precious, too great of cost—
Last wonder to awake the divine spark,
A lovely presence lighting Summer's dark;
Though dust your frame of flesh, such dust as makes
Blue radiance of March in hidden brakes. . . .
Pass from your body then, be what you will,
Whose light-foot walk outdanced the daffodil,
Since Time can but confirm you and fulfil
That hidden crescent power in you—Old Time,
Spoiler of pride, and towers, and breath, and rhyme,
Yet on the spirit impotent of power and will.

Turmut-Hoeing

I straightened my back from turmut-hoeing
   And saw, with suddenly opened eyes,
Tall trees, a meadow ripe for mowing,
   And azure June's cloud-circled skies.

Below, the earth was beautiful
   Of touch and colour, fair each weed,
But Heaven's high beauty held me still,
   Only of music had I need.

And the white-clad girl at the old farm,
  Who smiled and looked across at me,
Dumb was held by that strong charm
  Of cloud-ships sailing a foamless sea.

In a Ward

(To J. W. H.)

O wind that tosses free
  The children's hair;
Scatters the blossom of
  Apple and pear;
Blow in my heart, touch me,
  Gladden me here.

You have seen so many things—
  Blow in and tell
Tales of white sand and golden
  'Gainst the sea swell.
Bring me fine meadow-thoughts,
  Fresh orchard smell.

Here we must stare through glass
  To see the sun—
Stare at flat ceilings white
  Till day is done:
While you, sunshine, starshine,
  May out and run.

Blow in and bring us all
  Dear home-delight—
Green face of the Spring earth,
  Blue of deep night.
Blot each of our faces
  From the others' sight.

Camps

Out of the line we rest in villages
  Quiet indeed, where heal the spirit's scars;
But even so, lapped deep in sunshine and ease,
  We are haunted for ever by the shapes of wars.

Green in the sun they lie, secret, deserted,
   Lovely against the blue the summits show,
Where once the bright steel sang, the red blood spurted,
   And brave men cowed their terrors long ago.

By day their life was easy; but at night,
   Even now, one hears strange rustlings in the bush;
And, straining tensely doubtful ear and sight,
   The stealthy moving ere the sudden rush;

And flinches from the spear. War's just-bright embers
   That Earth still keeps and treasures for the pride
In sacrifice there shown; with love remembers
   The beauty and quick strength of men that died.

Who died as we may die, for Freedom, beauty
   Of common living, calmly led in peace,
Yet took the flinty road and hard of duty,
   Whose end was life abundant and increase.

But—when Heaven's gate wide opening receives us
   Victors and full of song, forgetting scars;
Shall we see to stir old memories, to grieve us,
   Heaven's never-yet-healed sores of Michael's wars?

Girl's Song

The tossing poplar in the wind
   Shows underleaf of silver-white;
The roughness of the wind unkind
   Torments her out of all delight.
But O that he were here
Whose blows and whose caresses alike were dear!

The great oak to the tearing blast
   Stands steady with strong arms held wide,
So over him my anger passed,
   When his rough usage hurt my pride.
But O that once again
I might arouse that passion, endure that pain!

Solace of Men

Sweet smelling, sweet to handle, fair of hue
   Tobacco is. The soldier everywhere
   Takes it as friend, its friendliness to share,
Whether in fragrant wreaths it mount faint blue

In dug-out low, or surreptitiously to
  Parapet in rimy night, from hidden lair
  Of sentry; staying hunger, stilling fear—
The old dreams of comfort bringing anew.
For from that incense grows the stuff of dreams,
  And in those clouds a drowsing man may find
  All that was ever sweet to his starved mind,
    Heart long denied—dear friends, hills, horses, trees,
Slopes of brown ploughland, sunset's fading gleams . . .
    The bane of care, the spur to memories.

Day-Boys and Choristers

(TO THE BOYS OF KING'S SCHOOL, GLOUCESTER, 1900-1905)

Under the shade of the great Tower
  Where pass the goodly and the wise,
Year in, year out, winter and summer,
  With scufflings and excited cries,
Football rages, not told in pages
  Of Fame whereof the wide world hears;
A battle of divided Empire—
  The day-boys and the choristers.

CHORUS

So here's to the room where the dark beams cross over,
  And here's to the cupboard where hides the cane;
The paddock and fives-court, great chestnut, tall tower—
  When Fritz stops his fooling we'll see them again.

Golf balls, tennis balls, cricket and footballs,
  Balls of all sizes and sorts were sent
Soaring by wall and arch and ivy
  High, high over to banishment.
(Poor owner that loses!) And oh! but the bruises,
  Scars, and red hacks to cover the brave
Shins of the boldest, when up and down playground
  Victory surged, Victory, edged like a wave.

CHORUS

So here's to the room where the dark beams cross over,
  And here's to the cupboard where hides the cane,
The paddock and fives-court, great chestnut, tall tower—
  When Fritz stops his fooling we'll see them again.

Little they knew, those boys, how in Flanders
    And plains of France, in another day
A trial dreadful of nerve and sinew
    For four long years should test alway
That playtime pluck, that yet should carry
    Them through Hell's during worst, and how
Europe should honour them, a whole world praise them,
    Though Death tore their bodies and laid them low.

CHORUS

So here's to the room where the dark beams cross over,
    And here's to the cupboard where hides the cane;
The paddock and fives-court, great chestnut, tall tower—
    When Fritz stops his fooling we'll see them again.

At Reserve Depot

When Spring comes here with early innocency
    Of pale high blue, they'll put Revally back.
The passers-by carelessly amused will see
    Breakfastless boys killing the patient sack.

And there will be manœuvres where the violet shows,
    Hiding its dark fervour, guarding its flame,
Where I shall lie and stare while the mystery grows
    Huge and more huge, till the Sergeant calls my name.

Toasts and Memories

(TO THE MEN OF THE 2/5 GLOUCESTER REGIMENT)

When once I sat in estaminets
    With trusty friends of mine,
We drank to folk in England
    And pledged them well in wine,

While thoughts of Gloucester filled us—
    Roads against windy skies
At sunset, Severn river,
    Red inn-blinds, country cries.

That stung the heart with sorrow
    And barbéd sweet delight
At Riez Bailleul, Laventie,
    At Merville, many a night.

Now I am over Channel
  I cannot help but think
Of friends who stifle longing
  With friendly food and drink.

"Where's Gurney now, I wonder,
  That smoked a pipe all day;
Sometimes that talked like blazes,
  Sometimes had naught to say? "

And I, at home, must wonder
  Where all my comrades are:
Those men whose Heart-of-Beauty
  Was never stained by War.

From the Window

Tall poplars in the sun
Are quivering, and planes,
Forgetting the day gone,
Its cold un-August rains;
But with me still remains
The sight of beaten corn,
Crushed flowers and forlorn,
The summer's wasted gains—
Yet pools in secret lanes
Abrim with heavenly blue
Life's wonder mirror anew.
I must forget the pains
Of yesterday, and do
Brave things—bring loaded wains
The bare brown meadows through,
I must haste, I must out and run,
Wonder, till my heart drains
Joy's cup, as in high champagnes
Of blue, where great clouds go on
With white sails free from stains
Full-stretched, on fleckless mains—
With captain's joy of some proud galleon.

Ypres—Minsterworth

(To F. W. H.)

Thick lie in Gloucester orchards now
　Apples the Severn wind
With rough play tore from the tossing
　Branches, and left behind
Leaves strewn on pastures, blown in hedges,
　And by the roadway lined.

And I lie leagues on leagues afar
　To think how that wind made
Great shoutings in the wide chimney,
　A noise of cannonade—
Of how the proud elms by the signpost
　The tempest's will obeyed—

To think how in some German prison
　A boy lies with whom
I might have taken joy full-hearted
　Hearing the great boom
Of Autumn, watching the fire, talking
　Of books in the half gloom.

O wind of Ypres and of Severn
　Riot there also, and tell
Of comrades safe returned, home-keeping
　Music and Autumn smell.
Comfort blow him and friendly greeting,
　Hearten him, wish him well!

Near Midsummer

Severn's most fair to-day!
See what a tide of blue
She pours, and flecked alway
With gold, and what a crew
Of seagulls snowy white
Float round her to delight
Villagers, travellers.
A brown thick flood is hers
In winter when the rains
Wash down from Midland plains,
Halting wayfarers,
Low meadows flooding deep
With torrents from the steep

Mountains of Wales and small
Hillocks of no degree—
Streams jostling to the sea;
(Wrangling yet brotherly).
Blue June has altered all—
The river makes its fall
With murmurous still sound,
Past Pridings faëry ground,
And steep-down Newnham cliff. . . .
O Boys in trenches, if
You could see what any may
(Escaping town for the day),
Strong Severn all aglow,
But tideless, running slow:
Far Cotswolds all a-shimmer,
Blue Bredon leagues away—
Huge Malverns, farther, dimmer . . .
Then you would feel the fire
Of the First Days inspire
You, when, despising all
Save England's, honour's call,
You dared the worst for her:
Faced all things without fear,
So she might stand alway
A free Mother of men;
High Queen as on this day.
There would flood through you again
The old faith, the old pride
Wherein our fathers died,
Whereby our land was builded and dignified.

Toussaints

(To J. W. H.)

Like softly clanging cymbals were
Plane-trees, poplars Autumn had
Arrayed in gloriously sad
Garments of beauty wind-astir;
It was the day of all the dead—

Toussaints. In sombre twos and threes
Between those coloured pillars went
Drab mourners. Full of presences
The air seemed . . . ever and anon rent
By a slow bell's solemnities.

The past year's gloriously dead
Came, folk dear to that rich earth
Had given them sustenance and birth,
Breath and dreams and daily bread,
Took labour-sweat, returned them mirth.

Merville across the plain gleamed white,
The thronged still air gave never a sound,
Only, monotonous untoned
The bell of grief and lost delight.
Gay leaves slow fluttered to the ground.

Sudden, that sense of peace and prayer
Like vapour faded. Round the bend
Swung lines of khaki without end. . . .
Common was water, earth and air;
Death seemed a hard thing not to mend.

The Stone-Breaker

(TO DOROTHY)

The early dew was still untrodden,
    Flawless it lay on flower and blade,
The last caress of night's cold fragrance
    A freshness in the young day made.

The velvet and the silver floor
    Of the orchard-close was gold inlaid
With spears and streaks of early sunlight—
    Such beauty makes men half afraid.

An old man at his heap of stones
    Turned as I neared his clinking hammer,
Part of the earth he seemed, the trees,
    The sky, the twelve-hour heat of summer.

"Fine marnen, zür!" And the earth spoke
    From his mouth, as if the field dark red
On our right hand had greeted me
    With words, that grew tall grain instead.

* * * *

Oh, years ago, and near forgot!
   Yet, as I walked the Flemish way,
An hour gone, England spoke to me
   As clear of speech as on that day;

Since peasants by the roadway working
   Hailed us in tones uncouth, and one
Turned his face toward the marching column,
   Fronted, took gladness from the sun.

And straight my mind was set on singing
   For memory of a wrinkled face,
Orchards untrodden, far to travel,
   Sweet to find in my own place.

Drifting Leaves

The yellow willow leaves that float
   Down Severn after Autumn rains
Take not of trouble any note—
   Lost to the tree, its joys and pains.

But man that has a thousand ties
   Of homage to his place of birth,
Nothing surrenders when he dies;
   But yearns for ever to his earth—

Red ploughlands, trees that friended him,
   Warm house of shelter, orchard peace.
In day's last rosy influence dim
   They flock to us without a cease;

Through fast-shut doors of olden houses
   In soundless night the dear dead come,
Whose sorrow no live folk arouses,
   Running for comfort hither home.

Though leaves on tide may idly range,
   Grounding at last on some far mire—
Our memories can never change:
   We are bond, we are ruled with Love's desire.

Contrasts

If I were on the High Road
   That runs to Malvern Town,
I should not need to read, to smoke,
   My fear of death to drown;
Watching the clouds, skies, shadows dappling
   The sweet land up and down.

But here the shells rush over,
   We lie in evil holes,
We burrow into darkness
   Like rabbits or like moles,
Men that have breathed the Severn air,
   Men that have eyes and souls.

To-day the grass runs over
   With ripples like the sea,
And men stand up and drink air
   Easy and sweet and free;
But days like this are half a curse,
   And Beauty troubles me.

The shadows under orchards there
   Must be as clear and black—
At Minsterworth, at Framilode—
   As though we had all come back;
Were out at making hay or tedding,
   Piling the yellow stack.

The gardens grow as freshly
   On Cotswold's green and white;
The grey-stone cottage colours
   Are lovely to the sight,
As we were glad for dreams there,
   Slept deep at home at night;

While here we die a dozen deaths
   A score of times a day;
Trying to keep up heart and not
   To give ourselves away.
"Two years longer," "Peace to-morrow,"
   "Some time yet," they say!

To F. W. H.

Ink black and lustreless may hold
  A passion full of living fire:
Spring's green the Autumn does enfold—
  Things precious hide their bright in the mire.

And a whole county's lovely pride
  In one small book I found that made
More real the pictured Severn side
  Than crash and shock of cannonade.

Beneath, more strong than that dread noise
  The talk I heard of trees and men,
The still low-murmuring Earth-voice . . .
  God send us dreams in peace again.

The Immortal Hour

(To Winnie)

I have forgotten where the pleasure lay
  In resting idle in the summer weather,
Waiting on Beauty's power my spirit to sway,
  Since Life has taken me and flung me hither;

Here where gray day to day goes dully on,
  So evenly, so grayly that the heart
Not notices nor cares that Time is gone
  That might be jewelled bright and set apart.

And yet, for all this weight, there stirs in me
  Such music of Joy when some perceivéd flower
Breaks irresistible this crust, this lethargy,
  I burn and hunger for that immortal hour

When Peace shall bring me first to my own home,
  To my own hills; I'll climb and vision afar
Great cloud-fleets line on line up Severn come,
  Where winds of Joy shall cleanse the stain of war.

To His Love

He's gone, and all our plans
   Are useless indeed.
We'll walk no more on Cotswold
   Where the sheep feed
   Quietly and take no heed.

His body that was so quick
   Is not as you
Knew it, on Severn river
   Under the blue
   Driving our small boat through.

You would not know him now . . .
   But still he died
Nobly, so cover him over
   With violets of pride
   Purple from Severn side.

Cover him, cover him soon!
   And with thick-set
Masses of memoried flowers—
   Hide that red wet
   Thing I must somehow forget.

Migrants

(TO MRS. TAYLOR)

No colour yet appears
On trees still summer fine,
The hill has brown sheaves yet,
Bare earth is hard and set;
But autumn sends a sign
In this as in other years.

For birds that flew alone
And scattered sought their food
Gather in whirring bands;—
Starlings, about the lands
Spring cherished, summer made good,
Dark bird-clouds soon to be gone.

But above that windy sound
A deeper note of fear
All daylight without cease

Troubles the country peace;
War birds, high in the air,
Airplanes shadow the ground.

Seawards to Africa
Starlings with joy shall turn,
War birds to skies of strife,
Where Death is ever at Life;
High in mid-air may burn
Great things that trouble day.

Their time is perilous,
Governed by Fate obscure;
But when our April comes
About the thatch-eaved homes,—
Cleaving sweet air, the sure
Starlings shall come to us.

Old Martinmas Eve

The moon, one tree, one star,
Still meadows far,
Enwreathed and scarfed by phantom lines of white.
November's night
Of all her nights, I thought, and turned to see
Again that moon and star-supporting tree.
If some most quiet tune had spoken then;
Some silver thread of sound; a core within
That sea-deep silentness, I had not known
Ever such joy in peace, but sound was none—
Nor should be till birds roused to find the dawn.

After Music

Why, I am on fire now, and tremulous
    With sense of Beauty long denied; the first
    Opening of floodgate to the glorious burst
Of Freedom from the Fate that limits us
To work in darkness pining for the light,
Thirsting for sweet untainted draughts of air,
Clouds sunset coloured, Music ... O Music's bare
White heat of silver passion fiercely bright!
While sweating at the foul task, we can taste
No Joy that's clean, no Love but something lets
It from its power; the wisest soul forgets
What's beautiful, or delicate, or chaste.
Orpheus drew me (as once his bride) from Hell.
If wisely, her or me, the Gods can tell.

The Target

I shot him, and it had to be
One of us! 'Twas him or me.
"Couldn't be helped," and none can blame
Me, for you would do the same.

My mother, she can't sleep for fear
Of what might be a-happening here
To me. Perhaps it might be best
To die, and set her fears at rest.

For worst is worst, and worry's done.
Perhaps he was the only son . . .
Yet God keeps still, and does not say
A word of guidance any way.

Well, if they get me, first I'll find
That boy, and tell him all my mind,
And see who felt the bullet worst,
And ask his pardon, if I durst.

All's a tangle. Here's my job.
A man might rave, or shout, or sob;
And God He takes no sort of heed.
This is a bloody mess indeed.

Twigworth Vicarage

(To A. H. C.)

Wakened by birds and sun, laughter of the wind,
A man might see all heart's desire by raising
His pillowed sleepy head (still apt for lazing
And drowsy thought)—but then a green most kind
Waved welcome, and the rifted sky behind
Showed blue, whereon cloud-ships full-sailed went racing,
Man to delight and set his heart on praising
The Maker of all things, bountiful-hearted, kind.

May Hill, that half-revealéd tree-clad thing,
   Maisemore's delightful ridge, where Severn flowing
   Nourished a wealth of lovely wild things blowing
     Sweet as the air—Wainlodes and Ashleworth
To northward showed, a land where a great king
     Might sit to receive homage from the whole earth.

Hospital Pictures

(TO THE NURSES OF WARD 24, BANGOUR WAR HOSPITAL, NEAR EDINBURGH)

1. LADIES OF CHARITY

With quiet tread, with softly smiling faces
   The nurses move like music through the room;
While broken men (known, technically, as "cases")
   Watch them with eyes late deep in bitter gloom,
As though the Spring were come with all the Graces,
   Or maiden April walked the ward in bloom.

Men that have grown forgetful of Joy's power,
And old before their time, take courtesy
So sweet of girl or woman, as if some flower
Most strangely fair of Spring were suddenly
Thick in the woods at Winter's blackest hour—
The gift unlocked for—lovely Charity.

Their anguish they forget, and, worse, the slow
Corruption of Joy's springs; now breathe again
The free breath was theirs so long ago.
Courage renewed makes mock at the old pain.
Life's loveliness brings tears, and a new glow.
Somehow their sacrifice seems not in vain.

2. DUST

Lying awake in the ward
Long hours as any must,
I wonder where the dust
Comes from, the Dust, the Dust!
That makes their life so hard,—
The nurses, who must rub
The soon appearing crust
Of green on the bright knob.

And little bits of fluff,
Dull white upon the floor,
Most soft, most curious stuff
That sidles to the door
When no one sees, and makes
Deep wrinkles and heart-breaks;
Light sighs and curses rough.

Oh! if a scientist
Of warm and kindly heart
Should live a while apart,
(Old Satan's tail to twist,)
Poring on crucibles,
Vessels uncanny, till
He won at last to Hell's
Grand secret of ill-will—
How Fluff comes and how Dust,

Then nurses all would paint
Cheeks pretty for his sake;
Or stay in prayer awake
All night for that great Saint
Of Cleanliness, that bright
Devoted anchorite;
Brave champion and true knight.

3. "ABERDONIAN"

A soldier looked at me with blue hawk-eyes,
With kindly glances sorrow had made wise,
And talked till all I'd ever read in books
Melted to ashes in his burning looks;
And poets I'd despise and craft of pen,
If, while he told his coloured wonder-tales
Of Glasgow, Ypres, sea mist, spouting whales
(Alive past words or power of writing men),
My heart had not exulted in his brave
Air of the wild woodland and sea wave;
Or if, with each new sentence from his tongue,
My high-triumphing spirit had not sung
As in some April when the world was young.

4. COMPANION—NORTH-EAST DUGOUT

He talked of Africa,
    That fat and easy man.
I'd but to say a word,
    And straight the tales began.

And when I'd wish to read,
    That man would not disclose
A thought of harm, but sleep;
    Hard-breathing through his nose.

Then when I'd wish to hear
  More tales of Africa,
'Twas but to wake him up,
  And but a word to say

To press the button, and
  Keep quiet; nothing more;
For tales of stretching veldt,
  Kaffir and sullen Boer.

O what a lovely friend!
  O quiet easy life!
I wonder if his sister
  Would care to be my wife. . . .

5. THE MINER

Indomitable energy controlled
By Fate to wayward ends and to half use,
He should have given his service to the Muse,
To most men shy, to him, her humble soldier,
Frank-hearted, generous, bold.

Yet though his fate be cross, he shall not tire
Nor seek another service than his own:
For selfless valour and the primal fire
Shine out from him, as once from great Ulysses,
That king without a throne.

6. UPSTAIRS PIANO

O dull confounded Thing,
You will not sing
Though I distress your keys
With thumps; in ecstasies
Of wrath, at some mis-said
Word of the deathless Dead!

Chopin or dear Mozart,
How must it break your heart
To hear this Beast refuse
The choice gifts of the Muse!
And turn your airy thought
With clumsiness to nought.

I am guilty too, for I
Have let the fine thing by;
And spoilt high graciousness
With a note more or less;
Whose wandering fingers know
Not surely where they go;
Whose mind most weak, most poor,
Your fire may not endure
That's passionate, that's pure.

And yet, and yet, men pale
(Late under Passchendaele
Or some such blot on earth)
Feel once again the birth
Of joy in them, and know
That Beauty's not a show
Of lovely things long past.

And stricken men at last
Take heart and glimpse the light,
Grow strong and comforted
With eyes that challenge night,
With proud-poised gallant head,
And new-born keen delight.

Beethoven, Schumann, Bach:
These men do greatly lack,
And you have greatly given.
The fervent blue of Heaven
They will see with purer eyes—
Suffering has made them wise;
Music shall make them sweet.

If they shall see the stars
More clearly after their wars,
That is a good wage.
Yours is a heritage
Most noble and complete.
And if we, blind, have gone
Where a great glory shone,
Or deaf, where angels sang;
Forgive us, for you, too,
A little blind were, knew
Of weakness, once, the pang;
Of darkness, once, the fear.

And so, forgive this dear
Pig-hearted chest of strings,
And me, whose heart not sings
Nor triumphs as do yours
Within the Heavenly doors—
Walking the clear unhindered level floors.

Hidden Tales

The proud and sturdy horses
Gather their willing forces,
Unswerving make their courses
Over the brown
Earth that was mowing meadow
A month agone, where shadow
And light in the tall grasses
Quivered and was gone.

They spoil the nest of plover
And lark, turn up, uncover
The bones of many a lover
Unfamed in tales;
Arrows, old flints of hammers,
The rooks with hungry clamours
Hover around and settle
Seeking full meals.

Who knows what splendid story
Lies here, what hidden glory
Of brave defeat or victory
This earth might show.
None cares; the surging horses
Gather untiring forces
The keen-eyed farmer after
Guiding the plough.

Recompense

(TO THE MEN OF THE 2/5 GLOUCESTER REGIMENT)

I'd not have missed one single scrap of pain
That brought me to such friends, and them to me;
And precious is the smallest agony,
The greatest, willingly to bear again—
Cruel frost, night vigils, death so often ta'en
By Golgothas untold from Somme to Sea.
Duty's a grey thing; Friendship valorously

Rides high above all Fortune without stain.

Their eyes were stars within the blackest night
Of Evil's trial. Never mariner
Did trust so in the ever-fixéd star
As I in those. And so their laughter sounded—
Trumpets of Victory glittering in sunlight;
Though Hell's power ringed them in, and night surrounded.

The Tryst

(To W. M. C.)

In curtain of the hazel wood,
    From sunset to the clear-of-star,
An hour or more I feared, but stood—
    My lover's road was far.

Until within the ferny brake
    Stirred patter feet and silver talk
That set all horror wide awake—
    I fear the fairy folk . . .

That bind with chains and change a maid
    From happy smiling to a thing
Better in ground unhallowed laid
    Where holy bells not ring.

And whether late he came or soon
    I know not, through a rush of air
Along the white road under the moon
    I sped, till the golden square

Showed of the blind lamplighted; then,
    My hand on heart, I slackened, stood . . .
Though Robin be the man of men,
    I'll walk no more that wood.

The Plain

The plain's a waste of evil mire,
    And dead of colour, sodden-grey,
The trees are ruined, crumbled the spire
    That once made glad the innocent day.

The host of flowers are buried deep
   With friends of mine who held them dear;
Poor shattered loveliness asleep,
   Dreaming of April's covering there.

Oh, if the Bringer of Spring does care
   For Duty valorously done,
Then what sweet breath shall scent the air!
   What colour-blaze outbrave the sun!

Rumours of Wars

(To Mrs. Voynich)

On Sussex hills to-day
   Women stand and hear
The guns at work alway,
   Horribly, terribly clear.

The doors shake, on the wall
   The kitchen vessels move,
The brave heart not at all
   May soothe its tortured love,

Nor hide from truth, nor find
   Comfort in lies. No prayer
May calm. All's naught. The mind
   Waits on the throbbing air.

The frighted day grows dark.
   None dares to speak. The gloom
Makes bright and brighter the spark
   Of fire in the still room.

A crazy door shakes free. . . .
   "Dear God!" They stand, they stare . . .
A shape eyes cannot see
   Troubles blank darkness there.

She knows, and must go pray
   Numb-hearted by the bed
That was his own alway . . .
   The throbbing hurts her head.

"On Rest"

(TO THE MEN OF THE 2/5 GLOUCESTER REGIMENT)

It's a King's life, a life fit for a King!
To lie safe sheltered in some old hay-loft
Night long, on golden straw, and warm and soft,
Unroused; to hear through dreams dawn's thrushes sing
"Revally"—drowse again; then wake to find
The bright sun through the broken tiles thick-streaming.
"Revally" real: and there's an end to dreaming.
"Up, Boys, and Out!" Then O what green, what still
Peace in the orchard, deep and sweet and kind,
Shattered abruptly—splashing water, shout
On shout of sport, and cookhouse vessels banging,
Dixie against dixie musically clanging.—
The farmer's wife, searching for eggs, 'midst all
Dear farmhouse cries. A stroll: and then "Breakfast's up."
Porridge and bacon! Tea out of a real cup
(Borrowed). First day on Rest, a Festival
Of mirth, laughter in safety, a still air.
"No whizzbangs," "crumps" to fear, nothing to mind,
Danger and the thick brown mud behind,
An end to wiring, digging, end to care.
Now wonders begin, Sergeants with the crowd
Mix; Corporals, Lance-Corporals, little proud,
Authority forgotten, all goes well
In this our Commonwealth, with tales to tell,
Smokes to exchange, letters of price to read,
Letters of friends more sweet than daily bread.
The Sergeant-major sheathes his claws and lies
Smoking at length, content deep in his eyes.
Officers like brothers chaff and smile—
Salutes forgotten, etiquette the while,
Comrades and brothers all, one friendly band.
Now through the orchard (sun-dried of dewfall) in
And out the trees the noisy sports begin.
He that is proud of body runs, leaps, turns
Somersaults, hand-turns; the licensed jester flings
Javelins of blunt wit may bruise not pierce;
Ragtimes and any scrap of nonsense sings.
All's equal now. It's Rest, none cares, none escapes
The hurtless battering of those kindly japes.
Noon comes, the estaminets open welcome doors,
Men drift along the roads in three and fours,
Enter those cool-paven rooms, and sit
Waiting; many there are to serve, Madame

Forces her way with glasses, all ignores
The impatient clamour of that thirsty jam,
The outcries, catcalls, queries, doubtful wit,
Alike. Newspapers come, "Journal, m'sieur?"
"What's the news?" "Anything fresh, boy?" "Tell us what's new."
Dinner, perhaps a snooze, perhaps a stroll.
Tea, letters (most like), rations to divide
(Third of a loaf, half, if luck's our way).
No work, no work, no work! A lovely day!
Down the main street men loiter side by side.
So day goes on blue-domed till the west's afire
With the sun just sunken, though we cannot see,
Hidden in green, the fall of majesty.
Our hearts are lifted up, fierce with desire
But once again to see the ricks, the farms,
Blue roads, still trees of home in the rich glow;
Life's pageant fading slower and more slow
Till Peace folds all things in with tender arms.
The last stroll in the orchard ends, the last
Candles are lit in bivvy and barn and cart,
Where comrades talking lie, comfort at heart,
Gladder for danger shared in the hard past,
The stars grow bright 'gainst Heaven's still-deepening blue,
Lights in the orchard die. "I wonder how
Mother is keeping: she must be sleepy now
As we, yet may be wondering all night through."

Dicky

(To his Memory)

They found him when the day
Was yet but gloom;
Six feet of scarréd clay
Was ample room
And wide enough domain for all desires
For him, whose glowing eyes
Made mock at lethargies,
Were not a moment still;—
Can Death, all slayer, kill
The fervent source of those exultant fires?
Nay, not so;
Somewhere that glow
And starry shine so clear astonishes yet
The wondering spirits as they come and go.
Eyes that nor they nor we shall ever forget.

                                                      Omiecourt.

The Day of Victory

(TO MY CITY)

The dull dispiriting November weather
Hung like a blight on town and tower and tree,
Hardly was Beauty anywhere to see
Save—how fine rain (together
With spare last leaves of creepers once showed wet
As it were, with blood of some high-making passion,)
Drifted slow and slow. . . .
But steadily aglow
The City was, beneath its grey, and set
Strong-mooded above the day's inclemency.

Flaunting from houses, over the rejoicing crowd,
Flags waved; that told how nation against nation
Should war no more, their wounds tending awhile:—
The sullen vanquished; Victors with heads bowed.
And still the bells from the square towers pealed Victory,
The whole time cried Victory, Victory flew
Banners invisible argent; Music intangible
A glory of spirit wandered the wide air through.
All knew it, nothing mean of fire or common
Ran in men's minds; none so poor but knew
Some touch of sacred wonder, noble wonder,—
Thought's surface moving under;
Life's texture coarse transfiguring through and through.

Joking, friendly-quarrelling, holiday-making,
Eddying hither, thither, without stay
That concourse went, squibs, crackers, squibbing, cracking—
Laughter gay
All common-jovial noises sounded, bugles triumphing masterful, strident,
        clear above all,
Hail fellow, cat-call . . .
Yet one discerned
A new spirit learnt of pain, some great
Acceptance out of hard endurance learned
And truly; wrested bare of hand from Fate.
The soldier from his body slips the pack,
Staggers, relaxes, crouches, then lies back,
Glad for the end of torment. Here was more.

A sense of consummation undeserved,
Desire fulfilled beyond dreams, completion
Humbly accepted,—a proud and grateful nation
Took the reward of purpose had not swerved,
But steadily before
Saw out, with equal mind, through alternation
Of hope and doubt—a four-year purge of fire
Changing with sore
Travail the flawed spirit, cleansing desire.

And glad was I:
Glad—who had seen
By Somme and Ancre too many comrades lie.
It was as if the Woman's spirit moved
That multitude, never of Man that pays
So lightly for the treasure of his days—
Of some woman that too greatly had beloved
Yet, willing, half her care of life foregone;
Best half of being losing with her son,
Beloved, beautiful, born-of-agony One....

The dull skies wept still. Drooped suddenly
Flags all. No triumph there.
Belgium, the Stars and Stripes, Gaul, Italy,
Britain, assured Mistress, Queen of the Sea,
Forlorn colours showed; rags glory-bare.
Night came, starless, to blur all things over
That strange assort of Life;
Sister, and lover,
Brother, child, wife,
Parent—each with his thought, careless or passioned,
Of those who gave their frames of flesh to cover
From spoil their land and folk, desperately fashioned
Fate stubborn to their will.

Rain fell, miserably, miserably, and still
The strange crowd clamoured till late, eddied, clamoured,
Mixed, mused, drifted. . . . The Day of Victory.

Passionate Earth

(To J. W. H.)

Where the new-turned ploughland runs to clean
Edges of sudden grass-land, lovely, green—
Music, music clings, music exhales,
And inmost fragrance of a thousand tales.

There the heart lifts, the soul takes flight to sing
High at Heaven-gate; but loth for entering
Lest there such brown and green it never find;
Nor feel the sting
Of such a beauty left so far behind.

The Poplar

(TO MICKY)

A tall slim poplar
    That dances in
A hidden corner
    Of the old garden,
What is it in you
    Makes communion
With this wind of Autumn,
    The clouds, the sun?

You must be lonely
    Amidst round trees
With their matron-figures
    And stubborn knees,
Casting hard glances
    Of keen despite
On the lone girl that dances
    Silvery white.

But you are dearer
    To sky and earth
Than lime-trees, plane-trees
    Of meaner birth.
Your sweet shy beauty
    Dearer to us
Than tree-folk, worthy,
    Censorious.

Down Commercial Road (*Gloucester*)

(TO MY MOTHER)

When I was small and packed with tales of desert islands far
    My mother took me walking in a grey ugly street,
But there the sea-wind met us with a jolly smell of tar,
    A sailorman went past to town with slow rolling gait;
        And Gloucester she's famous in story.

The trees and shining sky of June were good enough to see,
   Better than books or any tales the sailormen might tell—
But tops'le spars against the blue made fairyland for me;
   The snorting tug made surges like the huge Atlantic swell.
     And Gloucester she's famous in story.

Then thought I, how much better to sail the open seas
   Than sit in school at spelling-books or sums of grocers' wares.
And I'd have knelt for pity at any captain's knees
   To go see the banyan tree or white Arctic bears.
     And Gloucester she's famous in story.

O Gloucester men about the world that dare the seas to-day,
   Remember little boys at school a-studying their best
To hide somehow from Mother, and get clear away
   To where the flag of England flies prouder than the rest.
     And Gloucester she's famous in story.

From Omiecourt

O small dear things for which we fight—
   Red roofs, ricks crowned with early gold,
   Orchards that hedges thick enfold—
O visit us in dreams to-night!

Who watch the stars through broken walls
   And ragged roofs, that you may be
   Still kept our own and proudly free
While Severn from the Welsh height falls.

Le Coq Français

(TO RONALD)

After the biting cold of the outer night
It seemed—("Le Coq Français")—a palace of light,
And its low roof black-timbered was most fine
After the iron and sandbags of the line.
Easy it was to be happy there! Madame,
Frying a savoury mess of eggs and ham,
Talking the while: of the War, of the crops, her son
Who should see to them, and would, when the War was done.
Of battalions who had passed there, happy as we
To find a house so clean, such courtesy
Simple, sincere; after vigils of frost
The place seemed the seventh Heaven of comfort; lost
In miraculous strange peace and warmth we'd sit

Till the prowling police hunted us out of it—
Away from café noir, café au lait, vin blanc,
Vin rouge, citron, all that does belong
To the kindly shelter of old estaminets,
Nooked and cornered, with mirth of firelight ablaze—
Herded us into billets; where candles must show
Little enough comfort after the steady glow
Of that wonderful fireshine. We must huddle us close
In blankets, hiding all but the crimson nose,
To think awhile of home, if the frost would let
Thought flow at all; then sleep, sleep to forget
All but home and old rambles, lovely days
Of maiden April, glamorous September haze,
All darling things of life, the sweet of desire—
Castles of Spain in the deep heart of the fire.

The Fisherman of Newnham

(TO MY FATHER)

When I was a boy at Newnham,
    For every tide that ran
Swift on its way to Bollo,
    I wished I were a man
To sail out and discover
    Where such a tide began.

But when my strength came on me
    'Tis I must earn my bread:
My Father set me fishing
    By Frampton Hock, instead
Of wandering to the ocean—
    Wherever Severn led.

And now I've come to manhood,
    Too many cares have I
To think of gallivanting
    (A wife and child forbye).
So I must wonder ever
    Until time comes to die.

Then I shall question Peter
    Upon the heavenly floor,
What makes the tide in rivers—
    How comes the Severn bore,
And all things he will tell me
    I never knew before.

The Lock-Keeper

(To the Memory of Edward Thomas)

A tall lean man he was, proud of his gun,
Of his garden, and small fruit trees every one
Knowing all weather signs, the flight of birds,
Farther than I could hear the falling thirds
Of the first cuckoo. Able at digging, he
Smoked his pipe ever, furiously, contentedly.
Full of old country tales his memory was;
Yarns of both sea and land, full of wise saws
In rough fine speech; sayings his father had,
That worked a twelve-hour day when but a lad.
Handy with timber, nothing came amiss
To his quick skill; and all the mysteries
Of sail-making, net-making, boat-building were his.
That dark face lit with bright bird-eyes, his stride
Manner most friendly courteous, stubborn pride,
I shall not forget, not yet his patience
With me, unapt, though many a far league hence
I'll travel for many a year, nor ever find
A winter-night companion more to my mind,
Nor one more wise in ways of Severn river,
Though her villages I search for ever and ever.

The Revellers

I saw a silver-bright shield hang
Entangled in the topmost boughs
Of an old elm-tree, and a house
Dreaming; the while a small stream sang
A tune of broken silver by,
And laughed and wondered at the sky.

A thousand thousand silver lamps
Dared the bright moon of stars. O! who,
Wandering that silver quiet through,
Might heed the river-mists, dew-damps?
All Heaven exulted, but Earth lay
Breathless and tranced in peace alway.

From the orange-windowed tavern near
A song some ancient lover had—
When stars and longing made him mad—
Fashioned from wonder at his dear,
Rang out. Yet none there moves a limb

To see such stars as passioned him.

The loth moon left the twigs and gazed
Full-fronted at the road, the stream,
That all but tiniest tunes adream
Stilled, held breath at last amazed.
The farmers from their revel came;
But no stars saw, and felt no flame.

"*Annie Laurie*"

(To H. N. H.)

The high barn's lit by many a guttering flare
    Of flickering candle, dangerous—(hence forbidden)—
    To warm soft straw, whereby the cold floor's hidden,
On which we soon shall rest without a care.
War is forgotten. Gossip fills the air
    Of home, and laughter sounds beyond the midden
    Under the stars, where Youth makes Joy unchidden
Of gods or men, and mocks at sorrow there.
But hark! what sudden pure untainted passion
    Seizes us now, and stills the garrulous?
A song of old immortal dedication
        To Beauty's service and one woman's heart.
    No tears we show, no sign of flame in us
        This hour of stars and music set apart.

The Battalion Is Now On Rest

(To "La Comtesse")

Walking the village street, to watch the stars and find
Some peace like the old peace, some soothe for soul and mind;
The noise of laughter strikes me as I move on my way
Towards England—Westward—and the last glow of day.

And here is the end of houses. I turn on my heel,
And stay where those voices a moment made me feel
As I were on Cotswold, with nothing else to do
Than stare at the old houses, to taste the night-dew;

To answer friendly greetings from rough voices kind....
Oh, one may try for ever to be calm and resigned,
A red blind at evening sets the poor heart on fire—
Or a child's face, a sunset—with the old hot desire.

Photographs

(To Two Scots Lads)

Lying in dug-outs, joking idly, wearily;
   Watching the candle guttering in the draught;
Hearing the great shells go high over us, eerily
   Singing; how often have I turned over, and laughed

With pity and pride, photographs of all colours,
   All sizes, subjects: khaki brothers in France;
Or mothers' faces worn with countless dolours;
   Or girls whose eyes were challenging and must dance,

Though in a picture only, a common cheap
   Ill-taken card; and children—frozen, some
(Babies) waiting on Dicky-bird to peep
   Out of the handkerchief that is his home

(But he's so shy!). And some with bright looks, calling
   Delight across the miles of land and sea,
That not the dread of barrage suddenly falling
   Could quite blot out—not mud nor lethargy.

Smiles and triumphant careless laughter. O
   The pain of them, wide Earth's most sacred things!
Lying in dugouts, hearing the great shells slow
   Sailing mile-high, the heart mounts higher and sings.

But once—O why did he keep that bitter token
   Of a dead Love?—that boy, who, suddenly moved,
Showed me, his eyes wet, his low talk broken,
   A girl who better had not been beloved.

That County

Go up, go up your ways of varying love,
Take each his darling path wherever lie
The central fires of secret memory;
Whether Helvellyn tower the lakes above;
Or black Plinlimmon time and tempest prove;
   Or any English heights of bravery.
   I will go climb my little hills to see
Severn, and Malverns, May Hill's tiny grove.

No Everest is here, no peaks of power
   Astonish men. But on the winding ways
   White in the frost-time, blinding in full June blaze,
    A man may take all quiet heart's delight—
Village and quarry, taverns and many a tower
   That saw Armada beacons set alight.

Interval

To straight the back, how good; to see the slow
   Dispersed cloud-flocks of Heaven wandering blind
   Without a shepherd, feel caress the kind
Sweet August air, soft drifting to and fro
Meadow and arable.—Leaning on my hoe
   I searched for any beauty eyes might find.
   The tossing wood showed silver in the wind;
Green hills drowsed wakeful in the golden glow.

Yet all the air was loud with mutterings,
   Rumours of trouble strange in that rich peace,
   Where War's dread birds must practise without cease
    All that the stoutest pilot-heart might dare.
Death over dreaming life managed his wings,
   Droning dull song in the sun-satiate air.

De Profundis

If only this fear would leave me I could dream of Crickley Hill
   And a hundred thousand thoughts of home would visit my heart in sleep;
But here the peace is shattered all day by the devil's will,
   And the guns bark night-long to spoil the velvet silence deep.

O who could think that once we drank in quiet inns and cool
   And saw brown oxen trooping the dry sands to slake
Their thirst at the river flowing, or plunged in a silver pool
   To shake the sleepy drowse off before well awake?

We are stale here, we are covered body and soul and mind
   With mire of the trenches, close clinging and foul.
We have left our old inheritance, our Paradise behind,
   And clarity is lost to us and cleanness of soul.

O blow here, you dusk-airs and breaths of half-light,
   And comfort despairs of your darlings that long
Night and day for sound of your bells, or a sight
   Of your tree-bordered lanes, land of blossom and song.

Autumn will be here soon, but the road of coloured leaves
    Is not for us, the up and down highway where go
Earth's pilgrims to wonder where Malvern upheaves
    That blue-emerald splendour under great clouds of snow.

Some day we'll fill in trenches, level the land and turn
    Once more joyful faces to the country where trees
Bear thickly for good drink, where strong sunsets burn
    Huge bonfires of glory—O God, send us peace!

Hard it is for men of moors or fens to endure
    Exile and hardship, or the Northland grey-drear;
But we of the rich plain of sweet airs and pure,
    Oh! Death would take so much from us, how should we not fear?

The Tower

(To M. H.)

On the old road of Roman, on the road
Of chivalry and pride—the path to Wales
Famed in the chronicles and full of tales—
Westward I went, songs in my mouth, and strode
Free-bodied, light of heart,
Past many a heaped waggon with golden load,
And rumbling carrier's cart.
When, near the bridge where snorting trains go under
With noise of thunder,
I turned and saw
A tower stand, like an immortal law—

Permanent, past the reach of Time and Change,
Yet fair and fresh as any flower wild blown;
As delicate, as fair
As any highest tiny cloudlet sown
Faint in the upper air.
Fragile yet strong, a music that vision seemed.
Though all the land was fair, let the eye range
Whither it will
On plain or hill,
It must return where white the tower gleamed
Wonderful, irresistible, bubble-bright
In the morning light.
And then I knew, I knew why men must choose
Rather the dangerous path of arms than let
Beauty be broken
That is God's token,

The sign of Him; why hearts of courage forget
Aught but the need supreme
To follow honour and the perilous thing:
Scorning Death's sting;
Knowing Man's faith not founded on a dream.

POEMS FROM CAMP AND TRENCH BY ISAAC ROSENBERG

And like the artist who creates
From dying things what never dies. . . .
Fragment.

Daughters of War

Space beats the ruddy freedom of their limbs,
Their naked dances with man's spirit naked
By the root side of the tree of life
(The under side of things
And shut from earth's profoundest eyes).

I saw in prophetic gleams
These mighty daughters in their dances
Beckon each soul aghast from its crimson corpse
To mix in their glittering dances:
I heard the mighty daughters' giant sighs
In sleepless passion for the sons of valour
And envy of the days of flesh,
Barring their love with mortal boughs across—
The mortal boughs, the mortal tree of life.
The old bark burnt with iron wars
They blow to a live flame
To char the young green days
And reach the occult soul; they have no softer lure,
No softer lure than the savage ways of death.
We were satisfied of our lords the moon and the sun
To take our wage of sleep and bread and warmth—
These maidens came—these strong everliving Amazons,
And in an easy might their wrists
Of night's sway and noon's sway the sceptres brake,
Clouding the wild, the soft lustres of our eyes.

Clouding the wild lustres, the clinging tender lights;
Driving the darkness into the flame of day
With the Amazonian wind of them
Over our corroding faces
That must be broken—broken for evermore,
So the soul can leap out
Into their huge embraces.

Though there are human faces
Best sculptures of Deity,
And sinews lusted after
By the Archangels tall,
Even these must leap to the love-heat of these maidens
From the flame of terrene days,
Leaving grey ashes to the wind—to the wind.

One (whose great lifted face,
Where wisdom's strength and beauty's strength
And the thewed strength of large beasts
Moved and merged, gloomed and lit)
Was speaking, surely, as the earth-men's earth fell away;
Whose new hearing drank the sound
Where pictures, lutes, and mountains mixed
With the loosed spirit of a thought,
Essenced to language thus—

"My sisters force their males
From the doomed earth, from the doomed glee
And hankering of hearts.
Frail hands gleam up through the human quagmire, and lips of ash
Seem to wail, as in sad faded paintings
Far-sunken and strange.
My sisters have their males
Clean of the dust of old days
That clings about those white hands
And yearns in those voices sad:
But these shall not see them,
Or think of them in any days or years;
They are my sisters' lovers in other days and years."

On Receiving the First News of the War

Snow is a strange white word;
No ice or frost
Has asked of bud or bird
For Winter's cost.

Yet ice and frost and snow
From earth to sky
This Summer land doth know;
No man knows why.

In all men's hearts it is:
Some spirit old
Hath turned with malign kiss
Our lives to mould.

Red fangs have torn His face,
God's blood is shed:
He mourns from His lone place
His children dead.

O ancient crimson curse!
Corrode, consume;
Give back this universe
Its pristine bloom.

CAPE TOWN, 1914.

Spring, 1916

Slow, rigid, is this masquerade
That passes as through a difficult air:
Heavily—heavily passes.
What has she fed on? Who her table laid
Through the three seasons? What forbidden fare
Ruined her as a mortal lass is?

I played with her two years ago,
Who might be now her own sister in stone;
So altered from her May mien,
When round the pink a necklace of warm snow
Laughed to her throat where my mouth's touch had gone.
How is this, ruined Queen?

Who lured her vivid beauty so
To be that strained chill thing that moves
So ghastly midst her young brood
Of pregnant shoots that she for men did grow?
Where are the strong men who made these their loves?
Spring! God pity your mood!

The Troop Ship

Grotesque and queerly huddled
Contortionists to twist
The sleepy soul to a sleep,
We lie all sorts of ways
And cannot sleep.
The wet wind is so cold,
And the lurching men so careless,
That, should you drop to a doze,
Winds' fumble or men's feet
Are on your face.

Marching

(AS SEEN FROM THE LEFT FILE).

My eyes catch ruddy necks
Sturdily pressed back—
All a red-brick moving glint.
Like flaming pendulums, hands
Swing across the khaki—
Mustard-coloured khaki—
To the automatic feet.

We husband the ancient glory
In these bared necks and hands.
Not broke is the forge of Mars;
But a subtler brain beats iron
To shoe the hoofs of death
(Who paws dynamic air now).
Blind fingers loose an iron cloud
To rain immortal darkness
On strong eyes.

Break of Day in the Trenches

The darkness crumbles away—
It is the same old druid Time as ever.
Only a live thing leaps my hand—
A queer sardonic rat—
As I pull the parapet's poppy
To stick behind my ear.
Droll rat, they would shoot you if they knew
Your cosmopolitan sympathies
(And God knows what antipathies).
Now you have touched this English hand
You will do the same to a German—
Soon, no doubt, if it be your pleasure
To cross the sleeping green between.
It seems you inwardly grin as you pass
Strong eyes, fine limbs, haughty athletes
Less chanced than you for life,
Bonds to the whims of murder,
Sprawled in the bowels of the earth,
The torn fields of France.
What do you see in our eyes
At the shrieking iron and flame
Hurled through still heavens?
What quaver—what heart aghast?

Poppies whose roots are in man's veins
Drop, and are ever dropping;
But mine in my ear is safe,
Just a little white with the dust.

Killed in Action

Your "Youth"[1] has fallen from its shelf,
And you have fallen, you yourself.
They knocked a soldier on the head,
I mourn the poet who fell dead.
And yet I think it was by chance,
By oversight you died in France.
You were so poor an outward man,
So small against your spirit's span,
That Nature, being tired awhile,
Saw but your outward human pile;
And Nature, who would never let
A sun with light still in it set,
Before you even reached your sky,
In inadvertence let you die.

Returning, We Hear the Larks

Sombre the night is:
And, though we have our lives, we know
What sinister threat lurks there.

Dragging these anguished limbs, we only know
This poison-blasted track opens on our camp—
On a little safe sleep.

But hark! Joy—joy—strange joy.
Lo! Heights of night ringing with unseen larks:
Music showering on our upturned listening faces.

Death could drop from the dark
As easily as song—
But song only dropped,
Like a blind man's dreams on the sand
By dangerous tides;
Like a girl's dark hair, for she dreams no ruin lies there,
Or her kisses where a serpent hides.

---

[1] "Youth," a volume of poems by I. Rosenberg.

The Destruction of Jerusalem by the Babylonian Hordes

They left their Babylon bare
Of all its tall men,
Of all its proud horses;
They made for Lebanon.

And shadowy sowers went
Before their spears to sow
The fruit whose taste is ash,
For Judah's soul to know.

They who bowed to the Bull god,
Whose wings roofed Babylon,
In endless hosts darkened
The bright-heavened Lebanon.

They washed their grime in pools
Where laughing girls forgot
The wiles they used for Solomon.
Sweet laughter, remembered not!

Sweet laughter charred in the flame
That clutched the cloud and earth,
While Solomon's towers crashed between
To a gird of Babylon's mirth.

The Burning of the Temple

Fierce wrath of Solomon,
Where sleepest thou? O see,
The fabric which thou won
Earth and ocean to give thee—
O look at the red skies.

Or hath the sun plunged down?
What is this molten gold—
These thundering fires blown
Through heaven, where the smoke rolled?
Again the great king dies.

His dreams go out in smoke.
His days he let not pass
And sculptured here are broke,
Are charred as the burnt grass,
Gone as his mouth's last sighs.

Home-Thoughts from France

Wan, fragile faces of joy,
Pitiful mouths that strive
To light with smiles the place
We dream we walk alive,

To you I stretch my hands,
Hands shut in pitiless trance
In a land of ruin and woe,
The desolate land of France.

Dear faces startled and shaken,
Out of wild dust and sounds
You yearn to me, lure and sadden
My heart with futile bounds.

The Immortals

I killed them, but they would not die.
Yea, all the day and all the night
For them I could not rest nor sleep,
Nor guard from them nor hide in flight!

Then in my agony I turned
And made my hands red in their gore.
In vain—for faster than I slew
They rose more cruel than before.

I killed and killed with slaughter mad;
I killed till all my strength was gone;
And still they rose to torture me,
For Devils only die for fun.

I used to think the Devil hid
In women's smiles and wine's carouse;
I called him Satan, Balzebub;
But now I call him dirty louse.

Louse Hunting

Nudes, stark and glistening,
Yelling in lurid glee. Grinning faces
And raging limbs
Whirl over the floor one fire;
For a shirt verminously busy
Yon soldier tore from his throat

With oaths
Godhead might shrink at, but not the lice,
And soon the shirt was aflare
Over the candle he'd lit while we lay.

Then we all sprang up and stript
To hunt the verminous brood.
Soon like a demons' pantomime
This plunge was raging.
See the silhouettes agape,
See the gibbering shadows
Mixed with the baffled arms on the wall.

See Gargantuan hooked fingers
Pluck in supreme flesh
To smutch supreme littleness.
See the merry limbs in that Highland fling
Because some wizard vermin willed
To charm from the quiet this revel
When our ears were half lulled
By the dark music
Blown from Sleep's trumpet.

Girl to Soldier on Leave

I love you, Titan lover,
My own storm-days' Titan.
Greater than the son of Zeus,
I know whom I would choose.

Titan—my splendid rebel—
The old Prometheus
Wanes like a ghost before your power:
His pangs were joys to yours.

Pallid days, arid and wan,
Tied your soul fast:
Babel-cities' smoky tops
Pressed upon your growth

Weary gyves. What were you
But a word in the brain's ways,
Or the sleep of Circe's swine?
One gyve holds you yet.

It held you hiddenly on the Somme
Tied from my heart at home:
O must it loosen now? I wish
You were bound with the old, old gyves.

Love! You love me—your eyes
Have looked through death at mine.
You have tempted a grave too much.
I let you—I repine.

Soldier: Twentieth Century

I love you, great new Titan!
Am I not you?
Napoleon and Cæsar
Out of you grew.

Out of unthinkable torture,
Eyes kissed by death,
Won back to the world again,
Lost and won in a breath,

Cruel men are made immortal.
Out of your pain born,
They have stolen the sun's power
With their feet on your shoulders worn.

Let them shrink from your girth,
That has outgrown the pallid days
When you slept like Circe's swine
Or a word in the brain's ways.

The Jew

Moses, from whose loins I sprung,
Lit by a lamp in his blood
Ten immutable rules, a moon
For mutable lampless men.

The blonde, the bronze, the ruddy,
With the same heaving blood,
Keep tide to the moon of Moses.
Then why do they sneer at me?

The Dying Soldier

"Here are houses," he moaned,
"I could reach, but my brain swims."
Then they thundered and flashed,
And shook the earth to its rims.

"They are gunpits," he gasped,
"Our men are at the guns.
Water! . . . Water! . . . Oh, water!
For one of England's dying sons."

"We cannot give you water,
Were all England in your breath."
"Water! . . . Water! . . . Oh, water!"
He moaned and swooned to death.

Dead Man's Dump

The plunging limbers over the shattered track
Racketed with their rusty freight,
Stuck out like many crowns of thorns,
And the rusty stakes like sceptres old
To stay the flood of brutish men
Upon our brothers dear.

The wheels lurched over sprawled dead
But pained them not, though their bones crunched;
Their shut mouths made no moan.
They lie there huddled, friend and foeman,
Man born of man, and born of woman;
And shells go crying over them
From night till night and now.

Earth has waited for them,
All the time of their growth
Fretting for their decay:
Now she has them at last!
In the strength of their strength
Suspended—stopped and held.

What fierce imaginings their dark souls lit?
Earth! Have they gone into you?
Somewhere they must have gone,
And flung on your hard back
Is their souls' sack,
Emptied of God-ancestralled essences.

Who hurled them out? Who hurled?

None saw their spirits' shadow shake the grass,
Or stood aside for the half used life to pass
Out of those doomed nostrils and the doomed mouth,
When the swift iron burning bee
Drained the wild honey of their youth.

What of us who, flung on the shrieking pyre,
Walk, our usual thoughts untouched,
Our lucky limbs as on ichor fed,
Immortal seeming ever?
Perhaps when the flames beat loud on us,
A fear may choke in our veins
And the startled blood may stop.

The air is loud with death,
The dark air spurts with fire,
The explosions ceaseless are.
Timelessly now, some minutes past,
These dead strode time with vigorous life,
Till the shrapnel called "An end!"
But not to all. In bleeding pangs
Some borne on stretchers dreamed of home,
Dear things, war-blotted from their hearts.

A man's brains splattered on
A stretcher-bearer's face;
His shook shoulders slipped their load,
But when they bent to look again
The drowning soul was sunk too deep
For human tenderness.

They left this dead with the older dead,
Stretched at the cross roads.

Burnt black by strange decay
Their sinister faces lie,
The lid over each eye;
The grass and coloured clay
More motion have than they,
Joined to the great sunk silences.

Here is one not long dead.
His dark hearing caught our far wheels,
And the choked soul stretched weak hands
To reach the living word the far wheels said;
The blood-dazed intelligence beating for light,

Crying through the suspense of the far torturing wheels
Swift for the end to break
Or the wheels to break,
Cried as the tide of the world broke over his sight,
"Will they come? Will they ever come?"
Even as the mixed hoofs of the mules,
The quivering-bellied mules,
And the rushing wheels all mixed
With his tortured upturned sight.

So we crashed round the bend,
We heard his weak scream,
We heard his very last sound,
And our wheels grazed his dead face.

In War

Fret the nonchalant noon
With your spleen
Or your gay brow,
For the motion of your spirit
Ever moves with these.

When day shall be too quiet,
Deaf to you
And your dumb smile,
Untuned air shall lap the stillness
In the old space for your voice—

The voice that once could mirror
Remote depths
Of moving being,
Stirred by responsive voices near,
Suddenly stilled for ever.

No ghost darkens the places
Dark to One;
But my eyes dream,
And my heart is heavy to think
How it was heavy once.

In the old days when death
Stalked the world
For the flower of men,
And the rose of beauty faded
And pined in the great gloom,

One day we dug a grave:
We were vexed
With the sun's heat.
We scanned the hooded dead:
At noon we sat and talked.

How death had kissed their eyes
Three dread noons since,
How human art won
The dark soul to flicker
Till it was lost again:

And we whom chance kept whole—
But haggard,
Spent—were charged
To make a place for them who knew
No pain in any place.

The good priest came to pray;
Our ears half heard,
And half we thought
Of alien things, irrelevant;
And the heat and thirst were great.

The good priest read: "I heard . . ."
Dimly my brain
Held words and lost. . . .
Sudden my blood ran cold. . . .
God! God! It could not be.

He read my brother's name;
I sank—
I clutched the priest.
They did not tell me it was he
Was killed three days ago.

What are the great sceptred dooms
To us, caught
In the wild wave?
We break ourselves on them,
My brother, our hearts and years.

The Dead Heroes

Flame out, you glorious skies,
Welcome our brave;
Kiss their exultant eyes;
Give what they gave.

Flash, mailed seraphim,
Your burning spears;
New days to outflame their dim
Heroic years.

Thrills their baptismal tread
The bright proud air;
The embattled plumes outspread
Burn upwards there.

Flame out, flame out, O Song!
Star ring to star;
Strong as our hurt is strong
Our children are.

Their blood is England's heart;
By their dead hands
It is their noble part
That England stands.

England—Time gave them thee;
They gave back this
To win Eternity
And claim God's kiss.

VERSES OF A V.A.D

By VERA M. BRITTAIN

Dedicated to the Memory of Roland Aubrey Leighton, Lieutenant, Worcestershire Regiment. Died of Wounds Near Hébuterne, December 23rd, 1915.

> "Good-bye, sweet friend. What matters it that you
> Have found Love's death in joy, and I in sorrow?
> For hand in hand, just as we used to do,
> We two shall live our passionate poem through
> On God's serene to-morrow."
>
> R. A. L.

Foreword

These poems, by a writer for whom I have literary hopes, belong very
clearly to that new and vigorous type of poetry which has sprung from the stress
of the last few years and has its root in things done and suffered rather than in
things merely imagined.

Until lately our very belief in the saying that the poet is born and not made
proved that we had completely accepted poetry as coming only from within,
spun, as it were, out of our inner consciousness, and either quite unhelped, or
else only partially helped, by active experiences from without. We have always
understood, of course, that such an experience as, for instance, the sudden
flashing upon us of a magnetic face as a stranger passes in the street might set
aglow a train of thought that would quicken and melt into feeling, and the
feeling would, in turn, need—and find—expression in poetry.

So far as this we have admitted that outward occurrences in the course of
our quickly flying days can become a source of poetical inspiration. But, in spite
of the pointing finger of Kipling, most of us clung desperately to the verse that
had its sole origin in imaginative emotion until the blaze of war in the world
illumined our souls and showed all of us that out of our simplest practical work
can be struck sparks of real and great and rare divine fire.

All the poems in this little book are the outcome of things very deeply felt.
It is very difficult for me to write of them because where there is pain uttered in
them, it has almost always been my pain as well as the author's. One or two of
the sonnets condense the expression of losses that have meant a life's upheaval.
One or two, again, are practically a concrete record of simple human things
observed and suffered and of duty strenuously done. Here there is no leisured
dreaming, but sheer experience, solid and stored up, like the honey that a bee's
labour has stored.

But this practical quality, while it has so much that makes it rich and
valuable, has also the one conspicuous disadvantage that the work is often done
under conditions of strain and turmoil that tell against perfection of method.
Some of these *Verses of a V.A.D.* were written in almost breathless intervals of
severe and devoted duty. The poem entitled "The German Ward" is especially
an example of this. In such circumstances, it is difficult to achieve any literary
ornamentation and least of all that particular kind of simpleness which is the
highest form of finished art. In the case of several of the poems, both these
qualities have been achieved; yet, because of the difficulties, I make an appeal
for considerateness and tender sympathy in judging these first shy flowers of the
heart and mind of a young girl who has worked unceasingly and self-
forgettingly for the good of others since the days of stress began, and who in her
personal destiny has suffered as, I hope, very few have suffered.

MARIE CONNOR LEIGHTON.

August 1914

God said, "Men have forgotten Me;
  The souls that sleep shall wake again,
And blinded eyes must learn to see."

So since redemption comes through pain
  He smote the earth with chastening rod,
And brought Destruction's lurid reign;

But where His desolation trod
  The people in their agony
Despairing cried, "There is no God."

SOMERVILLE COLLEGE, OXFORD.

St. Pancras Station, August 1915

One long, sweet kiss pressed close upon my lips,
  One moment's rest on your swift-beating heart,
And all was over, for the hour had come
    For us to part.

A sudden forward motion of the train,
  The world grown dark although the sun still shone,
One last blurred look through aching tear-dimmed eyes—
    And you were gone.

To a Fallen Idol

O you who sought to rend the stars from Heaven
  But rent instead your too-ambitious heart,
Know that with those to whom Love's joy is given
    You have not, nor can ever have, a part.

A nation's loyalty might have been your glory,
  And men have blessed your name from shore to shore,
But you have set the seal upon your story,
    And must go hence, alone for evermore.

To Monseigneur

(R.A.L., LIEUTENANT, WORCESTERS)

None shall dispute Your kingship, nor declare
  Another could have held the place You hold,
  For though he brought me finer gifts than gold,
And laid before my feet his heart made bare

Of all but love for me, and sighed despair
  If I but feigned my favours to withhold,
  And would repudiate as sadly cold
The proud and lofty manner that You wear,

He would not be my pure and stainless knight
  Of heart without reproach or hint of fear,
Who walks unscathed amid War's sordid ways
By base desire or bloodshed's grim delight,
  But ever holds his hero's honour dear—
Roland of Roncesvalles in modern days.

1ST LONDON GENERAL HOSPITAL, November 1915.

The Only Son

The storm beats loud, and you are far away,
        The night is wild,
On distant fields of battle breaks the day,
        My little child?

I sought to shield you from the least of ills
        In bygone years,
I soothed with dreams of manhood's far-off hills
        Your baby fears,

But could not save you from the shock of strife;
        With radiant eyes
You seized the sword and in the path of Life
        You sought your prize.

The tempests rage, but you are fast asleep;
        Though winds be wild
They cannot break your endless slumbers deep,
        My little child.

Perhaps——

(TO R.A.L. DIED OF WOUNDS IN FRANCE, DECEMBER 23RD, 1915)

Perhaps some day the sun will shine again,
  And I shall see that still the skies are blue,
And feel once more I do not live in vain,
  Although bereft of You.

Perhaps the golden meadows at my feet
  Will make the sunny hours of Spring seem gay,
And I shall find the white May blossoms sweet,
  Though You have passed away.

Perhaps the summer woods will shimmer bright,
   And crimson roses once again be fair,
And autumn harvest fields a rich delight,
   Although You are not there.

Perhaps some day I shall not shrink in pain
   To see the passing of the dying year,
And listen to the Christmas songs again,
   Although You cannot hear.

But, though kind Time may many joys renew,
   There is one greatest joy I shall not know
Again, because my heart for loss of You
   Was broken, long ago.
            1ST LONDON GENERAL HOSPITAL, *February 1916.*

A Military Hospital

A mass of human wreckage, drifting in
   Borne on a blood-red tide,
Some never more to brave the stormy sea
   Laid reverently aside,
And some with love restored to sail again
   For regions far and wide.
            1ST LONDON GENERAL HOSPITAL, *1916.*

Looking Westward

      "For a while the quiet body
      Lies with feet toward the Morn."
           HYMN 499, A. & M.

When I am dead, lay me not looking East,
   But towards the verge where daylight sinks to rest,
For my Beloved, who fell in War's dark year,
   Lies in a foreign meadow, facing West.

He does not see the Heavens flushed with dawn,
   But flaming through the sunset's dying gleam;
He is not dazzled by the Morning Star,
   But Hesper soothes him with her gentle beam.

He faces not the guns he thrilled to hear,
   Nor sees the skyline red with fires of Hell;
He looks for ever towards that dear home land
   He loved, but bade a resolute farewell.

So would I, when my hour has come for sleep,
   Lie watching where the twilight shades grow grey;
Far sooner would I share with him the Night
   Than pass without him to the Splendid Day.

Then and Now

"πάντα ῥει καὶ οὐδένα μένει"

Once the black pine-trees on the mountain side,
   The river dancing down the valley blue,
And strange brown grasses swaying with the tide,
   All spoke to me of you.

But now the sullen streamlet creeping slow,
   The moaning tree-tops dark above my head,
The weeds where once the grasses used to grow
   Tell me that you are dead.

May Morning

(*Note.*—At Oxford on May 1st a Latin hymn is sung at sunrise by the Magdalen choristers from the top of the tower.)

The rising sun shone warmly on the tower,
   Into the clear pure Heaven the hymn aspired
Piercingly sweet. This was the morning hour
When life awoke with Spring's creative power,
   And the old City's grey to gold was fired.

Silently reverent stood the noisy throng;
   Under the bridge the boats in long array
Lay motionless. The choristers' far song
Faded upon the breeze in echoes long.
   Swiftly I left the bridge and rode away.

Straight to a little wood's green heart I sped,
   Where cowslips grew, beneath whose gold withdrawn
The fragrant earth peeped warm and richly red;
All trace of Winter's chilling touch had fled,
   And song-birds ushered in the year's bright morn.

I had met Love not many days before,
   And as in blissful mood I listening lay
None ever had of joy so full a store.
I thought that Spring must last for evermore,
   For I was young and loved, and it was May.

* * * * *

Now it is May again, and sweetly clear
  Perhaps once more aspires the Latin hymn
From Magdalen tower, but not for me to hear.
I toil far distant, for a darker year
  Shadows the century with menace grim.

I walk in ways where pain and sorrow dwell,
  And ruin such as only War can bring,
Where each lives through his individual hell,
Fraught with remembered horror none can tell,
  And no more is there glory in the Spring.

And I am worn with tears, for he I loved
  Lies cold beneath the stricken sod of France;
Hope has forsaken me, by Death removed,
And Love that seemed so strong and gay has proved
  A poor crushed thing, the toy of cruel Chance.

Often I wonder, as I grieve in vain,
  If when the long, long future years creep slow,
And War and tears alike have ceased to reign,
I ever shall recapture, once again,
  The mood of that May morning, long ago.
                    1ST LONDON GENERAL HOSPITAL, *May 1916.*

The Two Travellers

      Beware!
You met two travellers in the town
Who promised you that they would take you down
The valley far away
To some strange carnival this Summer's day.
      Take care,
Lest in the crowded street
They hurry past you with forgetting feet,
      And leave you standing there.

Roundel

("DIED OF WOUNDS")

Because you died, I shall not rest again,
  But wander ever through the lone world wide,
Seeking the shadow of a dream grown vain
      Because you died.

I shall spend brief and idle hours beside
  The many lesser loves that still remain,
But find in none my triumph and my pride;

And Disillusion's slow corroding stain
  Will creep upon each quest but newly tried,
For every striving now shall nothing gain
      Because you died.

FRANCE, *February 1918.*

The Sisters Buried at Lemnos

("FIDELIS AD EXTREMUM")

O golden Isle set in the deep blue Ocean,
  With purple shadows flitting o'er thy crest,
I kneel to thee in reverent devotion
  Of some who on thy bosom lie at rest!

Seldom they enter into song or story;
  Poets praise the soldier's might and deeds of War,
But few exalt the Sisters, and the glory
  Of women dead beneath a distant star.

No armies threatened in that lonely station,
  They fought not fire or steel or ruthless foe,
But heat and hunger, sickness and privation,
  And Winter's deathly chill and blinding snow.

Till mortal frailty could endure no longer
  Disease's ravages and climate's power,
In body weak, but spirit ever stronger,
  Courageously they stayed to meet their hour.

No blazing tribute through the wide world flying,
  No rich reward of sacrifice they craved,
The only meed of their victorious dying
  Lives in the hearts of humble men they saved.

Who when in light the Final Dawn is breaking,
  Still faithful, though the world's regard may cease,
Will honour, splendid in triumphant waking,
  The souls of women, lonely here at peace.

O golden Isle with purple shadows falling
  Across thy rocky shore and sapphire sea,
I shall not picture these without recalling
  The Sisters sleeping on the heart of thee!
          H.M.H.S. "BRITANNIC," MUDROS, *October 1916.*

In Memoriam: *G.R.Y.T.*

(KILLED IN ACTION, APRIL 23RD, 1917)

I spoke with you but seldom, yet there lay
  Some nameless glamour in your written word,
  And thoughts of you rose often—longings stirred
By dear remembrance of the sad blue-grey
That dwelt within your eyes, the even sway
  Of your young god-like gait, the rarely heard
But frank bright laughter, hallowed by a Day
  That made of Youth Right's offering to the sword.

So now I ponder, since your day is done,
  Ere dawn was past, on all you meant to me,
  And all the more you might have come to be,
And wonder if some state, beyond the sun
  And shadows here, may yet completion see
Of intimacy sweet though scarce begun.
                MALTA, *May 1917.*

A Parting Word

(TO A FORTUNATE FRIEND)

If you should be too happy in your days
  And never know an hour of vain regret,
    Do not forget
That still the shadows darken all my ways.

If sunshine sweeter still should light your years,
  And you lose nought of all you dearly prize,
    Turn not your eyes
From my steep track of anguish and of tears.

And if perhaps your love of me is less
   Than I with all my need of you would choose,
Do not refuse
To love enough to lighten my distress.

And if the future days should parting see
   Of our so different paths that lately met,
      Remember yet
Those days of storm you weathered through with me.

MALTA, May 1917.

To My Brother[2]

(IN MEMORY OF JULY 1ST, 1916)

Your battle-wounds are scars upon my heart,
   Received when in that grand and tragic "show"
You played your part
   Two years ago,

And silver in the summer morning sun
   I see the symbol of your courage glow—
That Cross you won
   Two years ago.

Though now again you watch the shrapnel fly,
   And hear the guns that daily louder grow,
As in July
   Two years ago,

May you endure to lead the Last Advance
   And with your men pursue the flying foe
As once in France
   Two years ago.

Sic Transit——

(V.R., DIED OF WOUNDS, 2ND LONDON GENERAL HOSPITAL,
CHELSEA, JUNE 9TH, 1917)

I am so tired.
   The dying sun incarnadines the West,
And every window with its gold is fired,
   And all I loved the best

---

[2] Captain E. H. Brittain, M.C. Written four days before his death in action in the Austrian offensive on the Italian Front, June 15th, 1918.

Is gone, and every good that I desired
  Passes away, an idle hopeless quest;
Even the Highest whereto I aspired
  Has vanished with the rest.
I am so tired.

LONDON, *June 1917.*

To Them

I hear your voices in the whispering trees,
  I see your footprints on each grassy track,
Your laughter echoes gaily down the breeze—
  But you will not come back.

The twilight skies are tender with your smile,
  The stars look down with eyes for which I yearn,
I dream that you are with me all the while—
  But you will not return.

The flowers are gay in gardens that you knew,
  The woods you loved are sweet with summer rain,
The fields you trod are empty now, but you
  Will never come again.

June 1917.

Oxford Revisited

There's a gleam of sun on the grey old street
  Where we used to walk in the Oxford days,
And dream that the world lay beneath our feet
  In the dawn of a summer morning.

Now the years have passed, and it's we who lie
  Crushed under the burden of world-wide woe,
But the misty magic will never die
  From the dawn of an Oxford morning.

And the end delays, and perhaps no more
  I shall see the spires of my youth's delight,
But they'll gladden my eyes as in days of yore
  At the dawn of Eternal Morning.

June 1917.

That Which Remaineth

(IN MEMORY OF CAPTAIN E. H. BRITTAIN, M.C.)

Only the thought of a merry smile,
    The wistful dreaming of sad brown eyes—
A brave young warrior, face aglow
    With the light of a lofty enterprise.

Only the hope of a gallant heart,
    The steady strife for a deathless crown,
In Memory's treasures, radiant now
    With the gleam of a goal beyond renown.

Only the tale of a dream fulfilled,
    A strenuous day and a well-fought fight,
A fearless leader who laughed at Death,
    And the fitting end of a gentle knight.

Only a Cross on a mountain side,
    The close of a journey short and rough,
A sword laid down and a stainless shield—
    No more—and yet, is it not enough?

The German Ward

("INTER ARMA CARITAS")

When the years of strife are over and my recollection fades
    Of the wards wherein I worked the weeks away,
I shall still see, as a vision rising 'mid the War-time shades,
    The ward in France where German wounded lay.

I shall see the pallid faces and the half-suspicious eyes,
    I shall hear the bitter groans and laboured breath,
And recall the loud complaining and the weary tedious cries,
    And sights and smells of blood and wounds and death.

I shall see the convoy cases, blanket-covered on the floor,
    And watch the heavy stretcher-work begin,
And the gleam of knives and bottles through the open theatre door,
    And the operation patients carried in.

I shall see the Sister standing, with her form of youthful grace,
    And the humour and the wisdom of her smile,
And the tale of three years' warfare on her thin expressive face—
    The weariness of many a toil-filled while.

I shall think of how I worked for her with nerve and heart and mind,
  And marvelled at her courage and her skill,
And how the dying enemy her tenderness would find
  Beneath her scornful energy of will.

And I learnt that human mercy turns alike to friend or foe
  When the darkest hour of all is creeping nigh,
And those who slew our dearest, when their lamps were burning low,
  Found help and pity ere they came to die.

So, though much will be forgotten when the sound of War's alarms
  And the days of death and strife have passed away,
I shall always see the vision of Love working amidst arms
  In the ward wherein the wounded prisoners lay.

                                        FRANCE, *September 1917.*

The Troop-Train

(FRANCE, 1917)

As we came down from Amiens,
  And they went up the line,
They waved their careless hands to us,
  And cheered the Red Cross sign.

And often I have wondered since,
  Repicturing that train,
How many of those laughing souls
  Came down the line again.

To My Ward-Sister

NIGHT DUTY, DECEMBER 1917

Through the night-watches of our House of Sighs
  In capable serenity of mind
  You steadily achieve the tasks designed
With calm, half-smiling, interested eyes;
Though all-unknowing, confidently wise
  Concerning pain you never felt, you find
Content from uneventful years arise
  As you toil on, mechanically kind.

So thus far have your smooth days passed, but when
  The tempest none escape shall cloud your sky,
And Life grow dark around you, through your pain
You'll learn the meaning of your mercy then

To those who blessed you as you passed them by,
Nor seek to tread the untroubled road again.

FRANCE.

To Another Sister

I knew that you had suffered many things,
    For I could see your eyes would often weep
    Through bitter midnight hours when others sleep;
And in your smile the lurking scorn that springs
    From cruel knowledge of a love, once deep,
Grown gradually cold, until the stings
Pierce mercilessly of a past that clings
    Undying to your lonely path and steep.

So, loved and honoured leader, I would pray
    That hidden future days may hold in store
Some solace for your yearning even yet,
And in some joy to come you may forget
    The burdened toil you will not suffer more,
And see the War-time shadows fade away.

FRANCE, *1918.*

"Vengeance Is Mine"

(IN MEMORY OF THE SISTERS WHO DIED IN THE GREAT AIR RAID UPON HOSPITALS AT ÉTAPLES)

Who shall avenge us for anguish unnamable,
    Rivers of scarlet and crosses of grey,
Terror of night-time and blood-lust untamable,
    Hate without pity where broken we lay?

How could we help them, in agony calling us,
    Those whom we laboured to comfort and save,
How still their moaning, whose hour was befalling us,
    Crushed in a horror more dark than the grave?

Burning of canvas and smashing of wood above—
    Havoc of Mercy's toil—shall He forget
Us that have fallen, Who numbers in gracious love
    Each tiny creature whose life is man's debt?

Will He not hear us, though speech is now failing us—
    Voices too feeble to utter a cry?
Shall they not answer, the foemen assailing us,
    Women who suffer and women who die?

Who shall avenge us for anguish unnamable,
   Rivers of scarlet and crosses of grey,
Terror of night-time and blood-lust untamable,
   Hate without pity where broken we lay?

War

(THE GREAT GERMAN OFFENSIVE, MARCH—MAY 1918)

A night of storm and thunder crashing by,
   A bitter night of tempest and of rain—
Then calm at dawn beneath a wind-swept sky,
   And broken flowers that will not bloom again.

An age of Death and Agony and Tears,
   A cruel age of woe unguessed before—
Then peace to close the weary storm-wrecked years,
   And broken hearts that bleed for evermore.

FRANCE.

The Last Post

The stars are shining bright above the camps,
   The bugle calls float skyward, faintly clear;
Over the hill the mist-veiled motor lamps
   Dwindle and disappear.

The notes of day's good-bye arise and blend
   With the low murmurous hum from tree and sod,
And swell into that question at the end
   They ask each night of God—

Whether the dead within the burial ground
   Will ever overthrow their crosses grey,
And rise triumphant from each lowly mound
   To greet the dawning day.

Whether the eyes which battle sealed in sleep
   Will open to reveillé once again,
And forms, once mangled, into rapture leap,
   Forgetful of their pain.

But still the stars above the camp shine on,
   Giving no answer for our sorrow's ease,
And one more day with the Last Post has gone
   Dying upon the breeze.

ÉTAPLES, *1918.*

The Aspirant

(A PLEA)

Because I dare to stand outside the gate
    Of that high temple wherein Fame abides,
And loudly knock, too eager to await
    Whate'er betides,

May God forgive, since He alone can see
    The joys that others have but I must miss,
For how shall Compensation come to me
    If not through this?

THE WAR SONNETS OF RUPERT BROOKE

I. Peace

Now, God be thanked Who has matched us with His hour,
    And caught our youth, and wakened us from sleeping,
With hand made sure, clear eye, and sharpened power,
    To turn, as swimmers into cleanness leaping,
Glad from a world grown old and cold and weary,
    Leave the sick hearts that honour could not move,
And half-men, and their dirty songs and dreary,
    And all the little emptiness of love!

Oh! we, who have known shame, we have found release there,
    Where there's no ill, no grief, but sleep has mending,
        Naught broken save this body, lost but breath;
Nothing to shake the laughing heart's long peace there
    But only agony, and that has ending;
        And the worst friend and enemy is but Death.

II. Safety

Dear! of all happy in the hour, most blest
    He who has found our hid security,
Assured in the dark tides of the world that rest,
    And heard our word, 'Who is so safe as we?'
We have found safety with all things undying,
    The winds, and morning, tears of men and mirth,
The deep night, and birds singing, and clouds flying,
    And sleep, and freedom, and the autumnal earth.
We have built a house that is not for Time's throwing.
    We have gained a peace unshaken by pain for ever.
War knows no power. Safe shall be my going,

Secretly armed against all death's endeavour;
Safe though all safety's lost; safe where men fall;
And if these poor limbs die, safest of all.

III. The Dead

Blow out, you bugles, over the rich Dead!
    There's none of these so lonely and poor of old,
    But, dying, has made us rarer gifts than gold.
These laid the world away; poured out the red
Sweet wine of youth; gave up the years to be
    Of work and joy, and that unhoped serene,
    That men call age; and those who would have been,
Their sons, they gave, their immortality.

Blow, bugles, blow! They brought us, for our dearth,
    Holiness, lacked so long, and Love, and Pain.
Honour has come back, as a king, to earth,
    And paid his subjects with a royal wage;
And Nobleness walks in our ways again;
    And we have come into our heritage.

IV. The Dead

These hearts were woven of human joys and cares,
    Washed marvellously with sorrow, swift to mirth.
The years had given them kindness. Dawn was theirs,
    And sunset, and the colours of the earth.
These had seen movement, and heard music; known
    Slumber and waking; loved; gone proudly friended;
Felt the quick stir of wonder; sat alone;
    Touched flowers and furs and cheeks. All this is ended.

There are waters blown by changing winds to laughter
And lit by the rich skies, all day. And after,
    Frost, with a gesture, stays the waves that dance
And wandering loveliness. He leaves a white
    Unbroken glory, a gathered radiance,
A width, a shining peace, under the night.

V. The Soldier

If I should die, think only this of me:
    That there's some corner of a foreign field
That is for ever England. There shall be
    In that rich earth a richer dust concealed;
A dust whom England bore, shaped, made aware,
    Gave, once, her flowers to love, her ways to roam,

A body of England's, breathing English air,
   Washed by the rivers, blest by suns of home.

And think, this heart, all evil shed away,
   A pulse in the eternal mind, no less
      Gives somewhere back the thoughts by England given;
Her sights and sounds; dreams happy as her day;
   And laughter, learnt of friends; and gentleness,
      In hearts at peace, under an English heaven.

SELECTED POEMS OF ALAN SEEGER

The Aisne (1914-15)

We first saw fire on the tragic slopes
   Where the flood-tide of France's early gain,
Big with wrecked promise and abandoned hopes,
   Broke in a surf of blood along the Aisne.

The charge her heroes left us, we assumed,
   What, dying, they reconquered, we preserved,
In the chill trenches, harried, shelled, entombed,
   Winter came down on us, but no man swerved.

Winter came down on us. The low clouds, torn
   In the stark branches of the riven pines,
Blurred the white rockets that from dusk till morn
   Traced the wide curve of the close-grappling lines.

In rain, and fog that on the withered hill
   Froze before dawn, the lurking foe drew down;
Or light snows fell that made forlorner still
   The ravaged country and the ruined town;

Or the long clouds would end. Intensely fair,
   The winter constellations blazing forth—
Perseus, the Twins, Orion, the Great Bear—
   Gleamed on our bayonets pointing to the north.

And the lone sentinel would start and soar
   On wings of strong emotion as he knew
That kinship with the stars that only War
   Is great enough to lift man's spirit to.

And ever down the curving front, aglow
   With the pale rockets' intermittent light,
He heard, like distant thunder, growl and grow
   The rumble of far battles in the night,—

Rumors, reverberant, indistinct, remote,
    Borne from red fields whose martial names have won
The power to thrill like a far trumpet-note,—
    Vic, Vailly, Soupir, Hurtebise, Craonne . . .

Craonne, before thy cannon-swept plateau,
    Where like sere leaves lay strewn September's dead,
    I found for all dear things I forfeited
A recompense I would not now forego.

For that high fellowship was ours then
    With those who, championing another's good,
    More than dull Peace or its poor votaries could,
Taught us the dignity of being men.

There we drained deeper the deep cup of life,
    And on sublimer summits came to learn,
    After soft things, the terrible and stern,
After sweet Love, the majesty of Strife;

There where we faced under those frowning heights
    The blast that maims, the hurricane that kills;
    There where the watchlights on the winter hills
Flickered like balefire through inclement nights;

There where, firm links in the unyielding chain,
Where fell the long-planned blow and fell in vain—
    Hearts worthy of the honor and the trial,
We helped to hold the lines along the Aisne.

Champagne, (1914-15)

In the glad revels, in the happy fêtes,
    When cheeks are flushed, and glasses gilt and pearled
With the sweet wine of France that concentrates
    The sunshine and the beauty of the world,

Drink sometimes, you whose footsteps yet may tread
    The undisturbed, delightful paths of Earth,
To those whose blood, in pious duty shed,
    Hallows the soil where that same wine had birth.

Here, by devoted comrades laid away,
    Along our lines they slumber where they fell,
Beside the crater at the Ferme d'Alger
    And up the bloody slopes of La Pompelle,

And round the city whose cathedral towers
　　The enemies of Beauty dared profane,
And in the mat of multicolored flowers
　　That clothe the sunny chalk-fields of Champagne.

Under the little crosses where they rise
　　The soldier rests. Now round him undismayed
The cannon thunders, and at night he lies
　　At peace beneath the eternal fusillade . . .

That other generations might possess—
　　From shame and menace free in years to come—
A richer heritage of happiness,
　　He marched to that heroic martyrdom.

Esteeming less the forfeit that he paid
　　Than undishonored that his flag might float
Over the towers of liberty, he made
　　His breast the bulwark and his blood the moat.

Obscurely sacrificed, his nameless tomb,
　　Bare of the sculptor's art, the poet's lines,
Summer shall flush with poppy-fields in bloom,
　　And Autumn yellow with maturing vines.

There the grape-pickers at their harvesting
　　Shall lightly tread and load their wicker trays,
Blessing his memory as they toil and sing
　　In the slant sunshine of October days ...

I love to think that if my blood should be
　　So privileged to sink where his has sunk,
I shall not pass from Earth entirely,
　　But when the banquet rings, when healths are drunk,

And faces that the joys of living fill
　　Glow radiant with laughter and good cheer,
In beaming cups some spark of me shall still
　　Brim toward the lips that once I held so dear.

So shall one coveting no higher plane
　　Than nature clothes in color and flesh and tone,
Even from the grave put upward to attain
　　The dreams youth cherished and missed and might have known;

And that strong need that strove unsatisfied
  Toward earthly beauty in all forms it wore,
Not death itself shall utterly divide
  From the belovèd shapes it thirsted for.

Alas, how many an adept for whose arms
  Life held delicious offerings perished here,
How many in the prime of all that charms,
  Crowned with all gifts that conquer and endear!

Honor them not so much with tears and flowers,
  But you with whom the sweet fulfilment lies,
Where in the anguish of atrocious hours
  Turned their last thoughts and closed their dying eyes,

Rather when music on bright gatherings lays
  Its tender spell, and joy is uppermost,
Be mindful of the men they were, and raise
  Your glasses to them in one silent toast.

Drink to them—amorous of dear Earth as well,
  They asked no tribute lovelier than this—
And in the wine that ripened where they fell,
  Oh, frame your lips as though it were a kiss.
CHAMPAGNE, FRANCE, *July* 1915.

The Hosts

  Purged, with the life they left, of all
That makes life paltry and mean and small,
In their new dedication charged
With something heightened, enriched, enlarged,
That lends a light to their lusty brows
And a song to the rhythm of their tramping feet,
These are the men that have taken vows,
These are the hardy, the flower, the elite,—
These are the men that are moved no more
By the will to traffic and grasp and store
And ring with pleasure and wealth and love
The circles that self is the center of;
But they are moved by the powers that force
The sea forever to ebb and rise,
That hold Arcturus in his course,
And marshal at noon in tropic skies
The clouds that tower on some snow-capped chain
And drift out over the peopled plain.
They are big with the beauty of cosmic things.

Mark how their columns surge! They seem
To follow the goddess with outspread wings
That points toward Glory, the soldier's dream.
With bayonets bare and flags unfurled,
They scale the summits of the world
And fade on the farthest golden height
In fair horizons full of light.

    Comrades in arms there—friend or foe—
That trod the perilous, toilsome trail
Through a world of ruin and blood and woe
In the years of the great decision—hail!
Friend or foe, it shall matter nought;
This only matters, in fine: we fought.
For we were young and in love or strife
Sought exultation and craved excess:
To sound the wildest debauch in life
We staked our youth and its loveliness.
Let idlers argue the right and wrong
And weigh what merit our causes had.
Putting our faith in being strong—
Above the level of good and bad—
For us, we battled and burned and killed
Because evolving Nature willed,
And it was our pride and boast to be
The instruments of Destiny.
There was a stately drama writ
By the hand that peopled the earth and air
And set the stars in the infinite
And made night gorgeous and morning fair,
And all that had sense to reason knew
That bloody drama must be gone through.
Some sat and watched how the action veered—
Waited, profited, trembled, cheered—
We saw not clearly nor understood,
But yielding ourselves to the masterhand,
Each in his part as best he could,
We played it through as the author planned.

Maktoob

A shell surprised our post one day
  And killed a comrade at my side.
My heart was sick to see the way
    He suffered as he died.

I dug about the place he fell,
   And found, no bigger than my thumb,
A fragment of the splintered shell
     In warm aluminum.

I melted it, and made a mould,
   And poured it in the opening,
And worked it, when the cast was cold,
     Into a shapely ring.

And when my ring was smooth and bright,
   Holding it on a rounded stick,
For seal, I bade a Turco write
     Maktoob in Arabic.

Maktoob! "'Tis written!" . . . So they think,
   These children of the desert, who
From its immense expanses drink
     Some of its grandeur too.

Within the book of Destiny,
   Whose leaves are time, whose cover, space,
The day when you shall cease to be,
     The hour, the mode, the place,

Are marked, they say; and you shall not
   By taking thought or using wit
Alter that certain fate one jot,
     Postpone or conjure it.

Learn to drive fear, then, from your heart.
   If you must perish, know, O man,
'Tis an inevitable part
     Of the predestined plan.

And, seeing that through the ebon door
   Once only you may pass, and meet
Of those that have gone through before
     The mighty, the elite——

Guard that not bowed nor blanched with fear
   You enter, but serene, erect,
As you would wish most to appear
     To those you most respect.

So die as though your funeral
    Ushered you through the doors that led
Into a stately banquet hall
        Where heroes banqueted;

And it shall all depend therein
    Whether you come as slave or lord,
If they acclaim you as their kin
        Or spurn you from their board.

So, when the order comes: "Attack!"
    And the assaulting wave deploys,
And the heart trembles to look back
        On life and all its joys;

Or in a ditch that they seem near
    To find, and round your shallow trough
Drop the big shells that you can hear
        Coming a half mile off;

When, not to hear, some try to talk,
    And some to clean their guns, or sing,
And some dig deeper in the chalk—
        I look upon my ring:

And nerves relax that were most tense,
    And Death comes whistling down unheard,
As I consider all the sense
        Held in that mystic word.

And it brings, quieting like balm
    My heart whose flutterings have ceased,
The resignation and the calm
        And wisdom of the East.

I Have a Rendezvous with Death

    I have a rendezvous with Death
At some disputed barricade,
When Spring comes back with rustling shade
And apple-blossoms fill the air—
I have a rendezvous with Death
When Spring brings back blue days and fair.

It may be he shall take my hand
And lead me into his dark land
And close my eyes and quench my breath—
It may be I shall pass him still.
I have a rendezvous with Death
On some scarred slope of battered hill,
When Spring comes round again this year
And the first meadow-flowers appear.

God knows 'twere better to be deep
Pillowed in silk and scented down,
Where love throbs out in blissful sleep,
Pulse nigh to pulse, and breath to breath,
Where hushed awakenings are dear...
But I've a rendezvous with Death
At midnight in some flaming town,
When Spring trips north again this year,
And I to my pledged word am true,
I shall not fail that rendezvous.

Sonnet X

I have sought Happiness, but it has been
A lovely rainbow, baffling all pursuit,
And tasted Pleasure, but it was a fruit
More fair of outward hue than sweet within.
Renouncing both, a flake in the ferment
Of battling hosts that conquer or recoil,
There only, chastened by fatigue and toil,
I knew what came the nearest to content.
For there at least my troubled flesh was free
From the gadfly Desire that plagued it so;
Discord and Strife were what I used to know,
Heartaches, deception, murderous jealousy;
By War transported far from all of these,
Amid the clash of arms I was at peace.

Sonnet XI

On Returning to the Front after Leave

Apart sweet women (for whom Heaven be blessed),
Comrades, you cannot think how thin and blue
Look the leftovers of mankind that rest,
Now that the cream has been skimmed off in you.
War has its horrors, but has this of good—
That its sure processes sort out and bind

Brave hearts in one intrepid brotherhood
And leave the shams and imbeciles behind.
Now turn we joyful to the great attacks,
Not only that we face in a fair field
Our valiant foe and all his deadly tools,
But also that we turn disdainful backs
On that poor world we scorn yet die to shield—
That world of cowards, hypocrites, and fools.

Bellinglise

I

Deep in the sloping forest that surrounds
The head of a green valley that I know,
Spread the fair gardens and ancestral grounds
Of Bellinglise, the beautiful château.
Through shady groves and fields of unmown grass,
It was my joy to come at dusk and see,
Filling a little pond's untroubled glass,
Its antique towers and mouldering masonry.
Oh, should I fall to-morrow, lay me here,
That o'er my tomb, with each reviving year,
Wood-flowers may blossom and the wood-doves croon;
And lovers by that unrecorded place,
Passing, may pause, and cling a little space,
Close-bosomed, at the rising of the moon.

II

Here, where in happier times the huntsman's horn
Echoing from far made sweet midsummer eves,
Now serried cannon thunder night and morn,
Tearing with iron the greenwood's tender leaves.
Yet has sweet Spring no particle withdrawn
Of her old bounty; still the song-birds hail,
Even through our fusillade, delightful Dawn;
Even in our wire bloom lilies of the vale.
You who love flowers, take these; their fragile bells
Have trembled with the shock of volleyed shells,
And in black nights when stealthy foes advance
They have been lit by the pale rockets' glow
That o'er scarred fields and ancient towns laid low
Trace in white fire the brave frontiers of France.

May 22, 1916.

Liebestod

I who, conceived beneath another star,
Had been a prince and played with life, instead
Have been its slave, an outcast exiled far
From the fair things my faith has merited.
My ways have been the ways that wanderers tread
And those that make romance of poverty—
Soldier, I shared the soldier's board and bed,
And Joy has been a thing more oft to me
Whispered by summer wind and summer sea
Than known incarnate in the hours it lies
All warm against our hearts and laughs into our eyes.

I know not if in risking my best days
I shall leave utterly behind me here
This dream that lightened me through lonesome ways
And that no disappointment made less dear;
Sometimes I think that, where the hilltops rear
Their white entrenchments back of tangled wire,
Behind the mist Death only can make clear,
There, like Brunhilde ringed with flaming fire,
Lies what shall ease my heart's immense desire:
There, where beyond the horror and the pain
Only the brave shall pass, only the strong attain.

Truth or delusion, be it as it may,
Yet think it true, dear friends, for, thinking so,
That thought shall nerve our sinews on the day
When to the last assault our bugles blow:
Reckless of pain and peril we shall go,
Heads high and hearts aflame and bayonets bare,
And we shall brave eternity as though
Eyes looked on us in which we would seem fair—
One waited in whose presence we would wear,
Even as a lover who would be well-seen,
Our manhood faultless and our honor clean.

Resurgam

Exiled afar from youth and happy love,
    If Death should ravish my fond spirit hence
I have no doubt but, like a homing dove,
    It would return to its dear residence,
And through a thousand stars find out the road
Back into earthly flesh that was its loved abode.

A Message to America

You have the grit and the guts, I know;
You are ready to answer blow for blow
You are virile, combative, stubborn, hard,
But your honor ends with your own back-yard;
Each man intent on his private goal,
You have no feeling for the whole;
What singly none would tolerate
You let unpunished hit the state,
Unmindful that each man must share
The stain he lets his country wear,
And (what no traveller ignores)
That her good name is often yours.

You are proud in the pride that feels its might;
From your imaginary height
Men of another race or hue
Are men of a lesser breed to you:
The neighbor at your southern gate
You treat with the scorn that has bred his hate.
To lend a spice to your disrespect
You call him the "greaser". But reflect!
The greaser has spat on you more than once;
He has handed you multiple affronts;
He has robbed you, banished you, burned and killed;
He has gone untrounced for the blood he spilled;
He has jeering used for his bootblack's rag
The stars and stripes of the gringo's flag;
And you, in the depths of your easy-chair—
What did you do, what did you care?
Did you find the season too cold and damp
To change the counter for the camp?
Were you frightened by fevers in Mexico?
I can't imagine, but this I know—
You are impassioned vastly more
By the news of the daily baseball score
Than to hear that a dozen countrymen
Have perished somewhere in Darien,
That greasers have taken their innocent lives
And robbed their holdings and raped their wives.

Not by rough tongues and ready fists
Can you hope to jilt in the modern lists.
The armies of a littler folk
Shall pass you under the victor's yoke,
So be it a nation that trains her sons

To ride their horses and point their guns—
So be it a people that comprehends
The limit where private pleasure ends
And where their public dues begin,
A people made strong by discipline
Who are willing to give—what you've no mind to—
And understand—what you are blind to—
The things that the individual
Must sacrifice for the good of all.

    You have a leader who knows—the man
Most fit to be called American,
A prophet that once in generations
Is given to point to erring nations
Brighter ideals toward which to press
And lead them out of the wilderness.
Will you turn your back on him once again?
Will you give the tiller once more to men
Who have made your country the laughing-stock
For the older peoples to scorn and mock,
Who would make you servile, despised, and weak,
A country that turns the other cheek,
Who care not how bravely your flag may float,
Who answer an insult with a note,
Whose way is the easy way in all,
And, seeing that polished arms appal
Their marrow of milk-fed pacifist,
Would tell you menace does not exist?
Are these, in the world's great parliament,
The men you would choose to represent
Your honor, your manhood, and your pride,
And the virtues your fathers dignified?
Oh, bury them deeper than the sea
In universal obloquy;
Forget the ground where they lie, or write
For epitaph: "Too proud to fight."

    I have been too long from my country's shores
To reckon what state of mind is yours,
But as for myself I know right well
I would go through fire and shot and shell
And face new perils and make my bed
In new privations, if ROOSEVELT led;
But I have given my heart and hand
To serve, in serving another land,
Ideals kept bright that with you are dim;
Here men can thrill to their country's hymn,
For the passion that wells in the Marseillaise

Is the same that fires the French these days,
And, when the flag that they love goes by,
With swelling bosom and moistened eye
They can look, for they know that it floats there still
By the might of their hands and the strength of their will,
And through perils countless and trials unknown
Its honor each man has made his own.
They wanted the war no more than you,
But they saw how the certain menace grew,
And they gave two years of their youth or three
The more to insure their liberty
When the wrath of rifles and pennoned spears
Should roll like a flood on their wrecked frontiers.
They wanted the war no more than you,
But when the dreadful summons blew
And the time to settle the quarrel came
They sprang to their guns, each man was game;
And mark if they fight not to the last
For their hearths, their altars, and their past:
Yea, fight till their veins have been bled dry
For love of the country that *will* not die.

O friends, in your fortunate present ease
(Yet faced by the self-same facts as these),
If you would see how a race can soar
That has no love, but no fear, of war,
How each can turn from his private role
That all may act as a perfect whole,
How men can live up to the place they claim
And a nation, jealous of its good name,
Be true to its proud inheritance,
Oh, look over here and learn from FRANCE!

Introduction and Conclusion of a Long Poem

I have gone sometimes by the gates of Death
And stood beside the cavern through whose doors
Enter the voyagers into the unseen.
From that dread threshold only, gazing back,
Have eyes in swift illumination seen
Life utterly revealed, and guessed therein
What things were vital and what things were vain.
Know then, like a vast ocean from my feet
Spreading away into the morning sky,
I saw unrolled my vanished days, and, lo,
Oblivion like a morning mist obscured
Toils, trials, ambitions, agitations, ease,
And like green isles, sun-kissed, with sweet perfume

Loading the airs blown back from that dim gulf,
Gleamed only through the all-involving haze
The hours when we have loved and been beloved.

Therefore, sweet friends, as often as by Love
You rise absorbed into the harmony
Of planets singing round magnetic suns,
Let not propriety nor prejudice
Nor the precepts of jealous age deny
What Sense so incontestably affirms;
Cling to the blessed moment and drink deep
Of the sweet cup it tends, as there alone
Were that which makes life worth the pain to live.
What is so fair as lovers in their joy
That dies in sleep, their sleep that wakes in joy?
Caressing arms are their light pillows. They
That like lost stars have wandered hitherto
Lonesome and lightless through the universe,
Now glow transfired at Nature's flaming core;
They are the centre; constellated heaven
Is the embroidered panoply spread round
Their bridal, and the music of the spheres
Rocks them in hushed epithalamium.

* * * * *

I know that there are those whose idle tongues
Blaspheme the beauty of the world that was
So wondrous and so worshipful to me.
I call them those that, in the palace where
Down perfumed halls the Sleeping Beauty lay,
Wandered without the secret or the key.
I know that there are those, of gentler heart,
Broken by grief or by deception bowed,
Who in some realm beyond the grave conceive
The bliss they found not here; but, as for me,
In the soft fibres of the tender flesh
I saw potentialities of Joy
Ten thousand lifetimes could not use. Dear Earth,
In this dark month when deep as morning dew
On thy maternal breast shall fall the blood
Of those that were thy loveliest and thy best,
If it be fate that mine shall mix with theirs,
Hear this my natural prayer, for, purified
By that Lethean agony and clad
In more resplendent powers, I ask nought else
Than reincarnate to retrace my path,
Be born again of woman, walk once more

Through Childhood's fragrant, flowery wonderland
And, entered in the golden realm of Youth,
Fare still a pilgrim toward the copious joys
I savored here yet scarce began to sip;
Yea, with the comrades that I loved so well
Resume the banquet we had scarce begun
When in the street we heard the clarion-call
And each man sprang to arms—ay, even myself
Who loved sweet Youth too truly not to share
Its pain no less than its delight. If prayers
Are to be prayed, lo, here is mine! Be this
My resurrection, this my recompense!

Ode in Memory of the American Volunteers Fallen for France

(To have been read before the statue of Lafayette and Washington
in Paris, on Decoration Day, May 30, 1916)

I

Ay, it is fitting on this holiday,
Commemorative of our soldier dead,
When—with sweet flowers of our New England May
Hiding the lichened stones by fifty years made gray—
Their graves in every town are garlanded,
That pious tribute should be given too
To our intrepid few
Obscurely fallen here beyond the seas.
Those to preserve their country's greatness died;
But by the death of these
Something that we can look upon with pride
Has been achieved, nor wholly unreplied
Can sneerers triumph in the charge they make
That from a war where Freedom was at stake
America withheld and, daunted, stood aside.

II

Be they remembered here with each reviving spring,
Not only that in May, when life is loveliest,
Around Neuville-Saint-Vaast and the disputed crest
Of Vimy, they, superb, unfaltering,
In that fine onslaught that no fire could halt,
Parted impetuous to their first assault;
But that they brought fresh hearts and springlike too
To that high mission, and 'tis meet to strew
With twigs of lilac and spring's earliest rose
The cenotaph of those

Who in the cause that history most endears
Fell in the sunny morn and flower of their young years.

III

Yet sought they neither recompense nor praise,
Nor to be mentioned in another breath
Than their blue coated comrades whose great days
It was their pride to share—ay, share even to the death!
Nay, rather, France, to you they rendered thanks
(Seeing they came for honor, not for gain),
Who, opening to them your glorious ranks,
Gave them that grand occasion to excel,
That chance to live the life most free from stain
And that rare privilege of dying well.

IV

O friends! I know not since that war began
From which no people nobly stands aloof
If in all moments we have given proof
Of virtues that were thought American.
I know not if in all things done and said
All has been well and good,
Or if each one of us can hold his head
As proudly as he should,
Or, from the pattern of those mighty dead
Whose shades our country venerates to-day,
If we've not somewhat fallen and somewhat gone astray.
But you to whom our land's good name is dear,
If there be any here
Who wonder if her manhood be decreased,
Relaxed its sinews and its blood less red
Than that at Shiloh and Antietam shed,
Be proud of these, have joy in this at least,
And cry: "Now heaven be praised
That in that hour that most imperilled her,
Menaced her liberty who foremost raised
Europe's bright flag of freedom, some there were
Who, not unmindful of the antique debt,
Came back the generous path of Lafayette;
And when of a most formidable foe
She checked each onset, arduous to stem—
Foiled and frustrated them—
On those red fields where blow with furious blow
Was countered, whether the gigantic fray
Rolled by the Meuse or at the Bois Sabot,
Accents of ours were in the fierce mêlée;

And on those furthest rims of hallowed ground
Where the forlorn, the gallant charge expires,
When the slain bugler has long ceased to sound,
And on the tangled wires
The last wild rally staggers, crumbles, stops,
Withered beneath the shrapnel's iron showers:—
Now heaven be thanked, we gave a few brave drops;
Now heaven be thanked, a few brave drops were ours."

V

There, holding still, in frozen steadfastness,
Their bayonets toward the beckoning frontiers,
They lie—our comrades—lie among their peers,
Clad in the glory of fallen warriors,
Grim clusters under thorny trellises,
Dry, furthest foam upon disastrous shores,
Leaves that made last year beautiful, still strewn
Even as they fell, unchanged, beneath the changing moon;
And earth in her divine indifference
Rolls on, and many paltry things and mean
Prate to be heard and caper to be seen.
But they are silent, calm; their eloquence
Is that incomparable attitude;
No human presences their witness are,
But summer clouds and sunset crimson-hued,
And showers and night winds and the northern star.
Nay, even our salutations seem profane,
Opposed to their Elysian quietude;
Our salutations calling from afar,
From our ignobler plane
And undistinction of our lesser parts:
Hail, brothers, and farewell; you are twice blest, brave hearts.
Double your glory is who perished thus,
For you have died for France and vindicated us.

SELECTED POEMS OF ROBERT GRAVES

The Shadow of Death

Here's an end to my art!
  I must die and I know it,
With battle murder at my heart—
  Sad death for a poet!

Oh my songs never sung,
  And my plays to darkness blown!
I am still so young, so young,
  And life was my own.

Some bad fairy stole
  The baby I nursed:
Was this my pretty little soul,
  This changeling accursed?

To fight and kill is wrong—
  To stay at home wronger:
Oh soul, little play and song,
  I may father no longer!

Here's an end to my art!
  I must die and I know it,
With battle murder at my heart—
  Sad death for a poet!

The Morning Before the Battle

To-day, the fight: my end is very soon,
  And sealed the warrant limiting my hours:
I knew it walking yesterday at noon
  Down a deserted garden full of flowers.
. . . Carelessly sang, pinned roses on my breast,
  Reached for a cherry-bunch—and then, then, Death
Blew through the garden from the North and East
  And blighted every beauty with chill breath.

I looked, and ah, my wraith before me stood,
  His head all battered in by violent blows:
The fruit between my lips to clotted blood
  Was transubstantiate, and the pale rose
Smelt sickly, till it seemed through a swift tear-flood
  That dead men blossomed in the garden-close.

Limbo

After a week spent under raining skies,
  In horror, mud and sleeplessness, a week
Of bursting shells, of blood and hideous cries
  And the ever-watchful sniper: where the reek
Of death offends the living ... but poor dead
  Can't sleep, must lie awake with the horrid sound
That roars and whirs and rattles overhead

All day, all night, and jars and tears the ground;
When rats run, big as kittens: to and fro
   They dart, and scuffle with their horrid fare,
And then one night relief comes, and we go
   Miles back into the sunny cornland where
Babies like tickling, and where tall white horses
Draw the plough leisurely in quiet courses.

The Trenches

(*Heard in the Ranks*)

Scratches in the dirt?
No, that sounds much too nice.
Oh, far too nice.
Seams, rather, of a Greyback Shirt,
And we're the little lice
Wriggling about in them a week or two,
Till one day, suddenly, from the blue
Something bloody and big will come
Like—watch this fingernail and thumb!—
Squash! and he needs no twice.

(*Nursery Memories*)

I.—THE FIRST FUNERAL

(*The first corpse I saw was on the German wires, and couldn't be buried*)

The whole field was so smelly;
   We smelt the poor dog first:
His horrid swollen belly
   Looked just like going burst.

His fur was most untidy;
   He hadn't any eyes.
It happened on Good Friday
   And there was lots of flies.

And then I felt the coldest
   I'd ever felt, and sick,
But Rose, 'cause she's the oldest,
   Dared poke him with her stick.

He felt quite soft and horrid:
   The flies buzzed round his head
And settled on his forehead:
   Rose whispered: "That dog's dead.

"You bury all dead people,
   When they're quite really dead,
Round churches with a steeple:
   Let's bury this," Rose said.

"And let's put mint all round it
   To hide the nasty smell."
I went to look and found it—
   Lots, growing near the well.

We poked him through the clover
   Into a hole, and then
We threw brown earth right over
   And said: "Poor dog, Amen!"

(*Nursery Memories*)

II.—THE ADVENTURE

(*Suggested by the claim of a machine-gun team to have annihilated an enemy wire party: no bodies were found however*)

To-day I killed a tiger near my shack
Among the trees: at least, it must have been,
Because his hide was yellow, striped with black,
      And his eyes were green.

I crept up close and slung a pointed stone
With all my might: I must have hit his head,
For there he died without a twitch or groan,
      And he lay there dead.

I expect that he'd escaped from a Wild Beast Show
By pulling down his cage with an angry tear;
He'd killed and wounded all the people—so
      He was hiding there.

I brought my brother up as quick's I could
But there was nothing left when he did come:
The tiger's mate was watching in the wood
      And she'd dragged him home.

But, anyhow, I killed him by the shack,
'Cause—listen!—when we hunted in the wood
My brother found my pointed stone all black
      With the clotted blood.

(Nursery Memories)

III.—I HATE THE MOON

(After a moonlight patrol near the Brickstacks)

I hate the Moon, though it makes most people glad,
    And they giggle and talk of silvery beams—you know!
But *she* says the look of the Moon drives people mad,
    And that's the thing that always frightens me so.

I hate it worst when it's cruel and round and bright,
    And you can't make out the marks on its stupid face,
Except when you shut your eyelashes, and all night
    The sky looks green, and the world's a horrible place.

I like the stars, and especially the Big Bear
    And the W star, and one like a diamond ring,
But I *hate* the Moon and its horrible stony stare,
    And I know one day it'll do me some dreadful thing.

Big Words

"I've whined of coming death, but now, no more!
It's weak and most ungracious. For, say I,
Though still a boy if years are counted, why!
I've lived those years from roof to cellar-floor,
And feel, like grey-beards touching their fourscore,
Ready, so soon as the need comes, to die:
    And I'm satisfied.
For winning confidence in those quiet days
Of peace, poised sickly on the precipice side
Of Lliwedd crag by Snowdon, and in war
Finding it firmlier with me than before;
Winning a faith in the wisdom of God's ways
That once I lost, finding it justified
Even in this chaos; winning love that stays
And warms the heart like wine at Easter-tide;
    Having earlier tried
False loves in plenty; oh! my cup of praise
Brims over, and I know I'll feel small sorrow,
Confess no sins and make no weak delays
If death ends all and I must die to-morrow."

But on the firestep, waiting to attack,
He cursed, prayed, sweated, wished the proud words back.

The Dead Fox Hunter

We found the little captain at the head;
  His men lay well aligned.
We touched his hand—stone-cold—and he was dead,
  And they, all dead behind,
Had never reached their goal, but they died well;
They charged in line, and in the same line fell.

The well-known rosy colours of his face
  Were almost lost in grey.
We saw that, dying and in hopeless case,
  For others' sake that day
He'd smothered all rebellious groans: in death
His fingers were tight clenched between his teeth.

For those who live uprightly and die true
  Heaven has no bars or locks,
And serves all taste. . . . Or what's for him to do
  Up there, but hunt the fox?
Angelic choirs? No, Justice must provide
For one who rode straight and at hunting died.

So if Heaven had no Hunt before he came,
  Why, it must find one now:
If any shirk and doubt they know the game,
  There's one to teach them how:
And the whole host of Seraphim complete
Must jog in scarlet to his opening Meet.

It's a Queer Time

It's hard to know if you're alive or dead
When steel and fire go roaring through your head.

One moment you'll be crouching at your gun
Traversing, mowing heaps down half in fun:
The next, you choke and clutch at your right breast
No time to think—leave all—and off you go . . .
To Treasure Island where the Spice winds blow,
To lovely groves of mango, quince and lime—
Breathe no goodbye, but ho, for the Red West!
        It's a queer time.

You're charging madly at them yelling "Fag!"
When somehow something gives and your feet drag.
You fall and strike your head; yet feel no pain
And find . . . you're digging tunnels through the hay
In the Big Barn, 'cause it's a rainy day.
Oh springy hay, and lovely beams to climb!
You're back in the old sailor suit again.
          It's a queer time.

Or you'll be dozing safe in your dug-out—
A great roar—the trench shakes and falls about—
You're struggling, gasping, struggling, then . . . hullo!
Elsie comes tripping gaily down the trench,
Hanky to nose—that lyddite makes a stench—
Getting her pinafore all over grime.
Funny! because she died ten years ago!
          It's a queer time.

The trouble is, things happen much too quick;
Up jump the Bosches, rifles thump and click,
You stagger, and the whole scene fades away:
Even good Christians don't like passing straight
From Tipperary or their Hymn of Hate
To Alleluiah-chanting, and the chime
Of golden harps . . . and . . . I'm not well to-day . . .
          It's a queer time.

1915

I've watched the Seasons passing slow, so slow
In the fields between La Bassée and Bethune;
Primroses and the first warm day of Spring,
Red poppy floods of June,
August, and yellowing Autumn, so
To Winter nights knee-deep in mud or snow,
And you've been everything,

Dear, you've been everything that I most lack
In these soul-deadening trenches—pictures, books,
Music, the quiet of an English wood,
Beautiful comrade-looks,
The narrow, bouldered mountain-track,
The broad, full-bosomed ocean, green and black,
And Peace, and all that's good.

Over the Brazier

What life to lead and where to go
  After the War, after the War?
  We'd often talked this way before.
But I still see the brazier glow
That April night, still feel the smoke
And stifling pungency of burning coke.

I'd thought: "A cottage in the hills,
  North Wales, a cottage full of books,
  Pictures and brass and cosy nooks
And comfortable broad window-sills,
Flowers in the garden, walls all white.
I'd live there peacefully and dream and write."

But Willie said: "No, Home's no good:
  Old England's quite a hopeless place,
  I've lost all feeling for my race:
But France has given my heart and blood
Enough to last me all my life,
I'm off to Canada with my wee wife.

"Come with us, Mac, old thing," but Mac
  Drawled: 'No, a Coral Isle for me,
  A warm green jewel in the South Sea.
There's merit in a lumber shack,
And labour is a grand thing . . . but—
Give me my hot beach and my cocoanut.'

So then we built and stocked for Willie
  A log-hut, and for Mac a calm
  Rock-a-bye cradle on a palm—
Idyllic dwellings—but this silly
Mad War has now wrecked both, and what
Better hopes has my little cottage got?

July 1915.

An Old Twenty-Third Man

"Is that the Three-and-Twentieth, Strabo mine,
Marching below, and we still gulping wine?"
From the sad magic of his fragrant cup
The red-faced old centurion started up,
Cursed, battered on the table. "No," he said,
"Not that! The Three-and-Twentieth Legion's dead,
Dead in the first year of this damned campaign—

The Legion's dead, dead, and won't rise again.
Pity? Rome pities her brave lads that die,
But we need pity also, you and I,
Whom Gallic spear and Belgian arrow miss,
Who live to see the Legion come to this,
Unsoldierlike, slovenly, bent on loot,
Grumblers, diseased, unskilled to thrust or shoot.
O, brown cheek, muscled shoulder, sturdy thigh!
Where are they now? God! watch it struggle by,
The sullen pack of ragged ugly swine.
Is that the Legion, Gracchus? Quick, the wine!"
"Strabo," said Gracchus, "you are strange tonight.
The Legion is the Legion; it's all right.
If these new men are slovenly, in your thinking,
God damn it! you'll not better them by drinking.
They all try, Strabo; trust their hearts and hands.
The Legion is the Legion while Rome stands,
And these same men before the autumn's fall
Shall bang old Vercingetorix out of Gaul."

To Lucasta on Going to the War—For the Fourth Time

It doesn't matter what's the cause,
    What wrong they say we're righting,
A curse for treaties, bonds and laws,
    When we're to do the fighting!
And since we lads are proud and true,
    What else remains to do?
Lucasta, when to France your man
Returns his fourth time, hating war,
Yet laughs as calmly as he can
    And flings an oath, but says no more,
That is not courage, that's not fear—
Lucasta he's a Fusilier,
    And his pride sends him here.

Let statesmen bluster, bark and bray,
    And so decide who started
This bloody war, and who's to pay,
    But he must be stout-hearted,
Must sit and stake with quiet breath,
    Playing at cards with Death.
Don't plume yourself he fights for you;
It is no courage, love, or hate,
But let us do the things we do;
    It's pride that makes the heart be great;
It is not anger, no, nor fear—
Lucasta he's a Fusilier,

And his pride keeps him here.

Two Fusiliers

And have we done with War at last?
Well, we've been lucky devils both,
And there's no need of pledge or oath
To bind our lovely friendship fast,
By firmer stuff
Close bound enough.

By wire and wood and stake we're bound,
By Fricourt and by Festubert,
By whipping rain, by the sun's glare,
By all the misery and loud sound,
By a Spring day,
By Picard clay.

Show me the two so closely bound
As we, by the red bond of blood,
By friendship, blossoming from mud,
By Death: we faced him, and we found
Beauty in Death,
In dead men breath.

Goliath and David

(FOR D.C.T., KILLED AT FRICOURT, MARCH 1916)

Yet once an earlier David took
Smooth pebbles from the brook:
Out between the lines he went
To that one-sided tournament,
A shepherd boy who stood out fine
And young to fight a Philistine
Clad all in brazen mail. He swears
That he's killed lions, he's killed bears,
And those that scorn the God of Zion
Shall perish so like bear or lion.
But . . . the historian of that fight
Had not the heart to tell it right.

Striding within javelin range,
Goliath marvels at this strange
Goodly-faced boy so proud of strength.
David's clear eye measures the length;
With hand thrust back, he cramps one knee,
Poises a moment thoughtfully,

And hurls with a long vengeful swing.
The pebble, humming from the sling
Like a wild bee, flies a sure line
For the forehead of the Philistine;
Then . . . but there comes a brazen clink,
And quicker than a man can think
Goliath's shield parries each cast.
Clang! clang! and clang! was David's last.
Scorn blazes in the Giant's eye,
Towering unhurt six cubits high.
Says foolish David, "Damn your shield!
And damn my sling! but I'll not yield."
He takes his staff of Mamre oak,
A knotted shepherd-staff that's broke
The skull of many a wolf and fox
Come filching lambs from Jesse's flocks.
Loud laughs Goliath, and that laugh
Can scatter chariots like blown chaff
To rout; but David, calm and brave,
Holds his ground, for God will save.
Steel crosses wood, a flash, and oh!
Shame for beauty's overthrow!
(God's eyes are dim, His ears are shut.)
One cruel backhand sabre-cut
"I'm hit! I'm killed!" young David cries,
Throws blindly forward, chokes . . . and dies.
And look, spike-helmeted, grey, grim,
Goliath straddles over him.

The Last Post

The bugler sent a call of high romance—
"Lights out! Lights out!" to the deserted square.
On the thin brazen notes he threw a prayer,
"God, if it's *this* for me next time in France . . .
O spare the phantom bugle as I lie
Dead in the gas and smoke and roar of guns,
Dead in a row with the other broken ones
Lying so stiff and still under the sky,
Jolly young Fusiliers too good to die."

When I'm Killed

When I'm killed, don't think of me
Buried there in Cambrin Wood,
Nor as in Zion think of me
With the Intolerable Good.
And there's one thing that I know well,

I'm damned if I'll be damned to Hell!

So when I'm killed, don't wait for me,
Walking the dim corridor;
In Heaven or Hell, don't wait for me,
Or you must wait for evermore.
You'll find me buried, living-dead
In these verses that you've read.

So when I'm killed, don't mourn for me,
Shot, poor lad, so bold and young,
Killed and gone—don't mourn for me.
On your lips my life is hung:
O friends and lovers, you can save
Your playfellow from the grave.

A Dead Boche

To you who'd read my songs of War
    And only hear of blood and fame,
I'll say (you've heard it said before)
    "War's Hell!" and if you doubt the same,
Today I found in Mametz Wood
A certain cure for lust of blood:

Where, propped against a shattered trunk,
    In a great mess of things unclean,
Sat a dead Boche; he scowled and stunk
    With clothes and face a sodden green,
Big-bellied, spectacled, crop-haired,
Dribbling black blood from nose and beard.

The Next War

You young friskies who today
Jump and fight in Father's hay
With bows and arrows and wooden spears,
Playing at Royal Welch Fusiliers,
Happy though these hours you spend,
Have they warned you how games end?
Boys, from the first time you prod
And thrust with spears of curtain-rod,
From the first time you tear and slash
Your long-bows from the garden ash,
Or fit your shaft with a blue jay feather,
Binding the split tops together,
From that same hour by fate you're bound
As champions of this stony ground,

Loyal and true in everything,
To serve your Army and your King,
Prepared to starve and sweat and die
Under some fierce foreign sky,
If only to keep safe those joys
That belong to British boys,
To keep young Prussians from the soft
Scented hay of father's loft,
And stop young Slavs from cutting bows
And bendy spears from Welsh hedgerows.
    Another War soon gets begun,
A dirtier, a more glorious one;
Then, boys, you'll have to play, all in;
It's the cruellest team will win.
So hold your nose against the stink
And never stop too long to think.
Wars don't change except in name;
The next one must go just the same,
And new foul tricks unguessed before
Will win and justify this War.
Kaisers and Czars will strut the stage
Once more with pomp and greed and rage;
Courtly ministers will stop
At home and fight to the last drop;
By the million men will die
In some new horrible agony;
And children here will thrust and poke,
Shoot and die, and laugh at the joke,
With bows and arrows and wooden spears,
Playing at Royal Welch Fusiliers.

Escape

(*August* 6, 1916.—Officer previously reported died of wounds, now reported wounded: Graves, Captain R., Royal Welch Fusiliers.)

    ... But I *was* dead, an hour or more.
I woke when I'd already passed the door
That Cerberus guards, and half-way down the road
To Lethe, as an old Greek signpost showed.
Above me, on my stretcher swinging by,
I saw new stars in the subterrene sky:
A Cross, a Rose in bloom, a Cage with bars,
And a barbed Arrow feathered in fine stars.
I felt the vapours of forgetfulness
Float in my nostrils. Oh, may Heaven bless
Dear Lady Proserpine, who saw me wake,
And, stooping over me, for Henna's sake

Cleared my poor buzzing head and sent me back
Breathless, with leaping heart along the track.
After me roared and clattered angry hosts
Of demons, heroes, and policeman-ghosts.
"Life! life! I can't be dead! I won't be dead!
Damned if I'll die for any one!" I said. . . .

Cerberus stands and grins above me now,
Wearing three heads—lion, and lynx, and sow.
"Quick, a revolver! But my Webley's gone,
Stolen! . . . No bombs . . . no knife. . . . The crowd swarms on,
Bellows, hurls stones.... Not even a honeyed sop ...
Nothing. . . . Good Cerberus! . . . Good dog! . . . but stop!
Stay! . . . A great luminous thought . . . I do believe
There's still some morphia that I bought on leave."
Then swiftly Cerberus' wide mouths I cram
With army biscuit smeared with ration jam;

And sleep lurks in the luscious plum and apple.
He crunches, swallows, stiffens, seems to grapple
With the all-powerful poppy . . . then a snore,
A crash; the beast blocks up the corridor
With monstrous hairy carcase, red and dun—
Too late! for I've sped through.
O Life! O Sun!

Corporal Stare

Back from the line one night in June,
I gave a dinner at Bethune—
Seven courses, the most gorgeous meal
Money could buy or batman steal.
Five hungry lads welcomed the fish
With shouts that nearly cracked the dish;
Asparagus came with tender tops,
Strawberries in cream, and mutton chops.
Said Jenkins, as my hand he shook,
"They'll put this in the history book."
We bawled Church anthems *in choro*
Of Bethlehem and Hermon snow,
With drinking songs, a jolly sound
To help the good red Pommard round.
Stories and laughter interspersed,
We drowned a long La Bassée thirst—
Trenches in June make throats damned dry.
Then through the window suddenly,
Badge, stripes and medals all complete,
We saw him swagger up the street,

Just like a live man—Corporal Stare!
Stare! Killed last May at Festubert.
Caught on patrol near the Boche wire,
Tom horribly by machine-gun fire!
He paused, saluted smartly, grinned,
Then passed away like a puff of wind,
Leaving us blank astonishment.
The song broke, up we started, leant
Out of the window—nothing there,
Not the least shadow of Corporal Stare,
Only a quiver of smoke that showed
A fag-end dropped on the silent road.

The Assault Heroic

Down in the mud I lay,
Tired out by my long day
Of five damned days and nights,
Five sleepless days and nights, . . .
Dream-snatched, and set me where
The dungeon of Despair
Looms over Desolate Sea,
Frowning and threatening me
With aspect high and steep—
A most malignant keep.
My foes that lay within
Shouted and made a din,
Hooted and grinned and cried:
"Today we've killed your pride;
Today your ardour ends.
We've murdered all your friends;
We've undermined by stealth
Your happiness and your health.
We've taken away your hope;
Now you may droop and mope
To misery and to Death."
But with my spear of Faith,
Stout as an oaken rafter,
With my round shield of laughter,
With my sharp, tongue-like sword
That speaks a bitter word,
I stood beneath the wall
And there defied them all.
The stones they cast I caught
And alchemized with thought
Into such lumps of gold
As dreaming misers hold.
The boiling oil they threw

Fell in a shower of dew,
Refreshing me; the spears
Flew harmless by my ears,
Struck quivering in the sod;
There, like the prophet's rod,
Put leaves out, took firm root,
And bore me instant fruit.
My foes were all astounded,
Dumbstricken and confounded,
Gaping in a long row;
They dared not thrust nor throw.
Thus, then, I climbed a steep
Buttress and won the keep,
And laughed and proudly blew
My horn, "*Stand to! Stand to!*
Wake up, sir! Here's a new
Attack! Stand to! Stand to!"

SELECTED POEMS OF CHARLES SORLEY

[All the hills and vales along]

All the hills and vales along
Earth is bursting into song,
And the singers are the chaps
Who are going to die perhaps.
  O sing, marching men,
  Till the valleys ring again.
  Give your gladness to earth's keeping,
  So be glad, when you are sleeping.

Cast away regret and rue,
Think what you are marching to.
Little live, great pass.
Jesus Christ and Barabbas
Were found the same day.
This died, that went his way.
  So sing with joyful breath,
  For why, you are going to death.
  Teeming earth will surely store
  All the gladness that you pour.

Earth that never doubts nor fears,
Earth that knows of death, not tears,
Earth that bore with joyful ease
Hemlock for Socrates,
Earth that blossomed and was glad
'Neath the cross that Christ had,

Shall rejoice and blossom too
When the bullet reaches you.
  Wherefore, men marching
  On the road to death, sing!
  Pour your gladness on earth's head,
  So be merry, so be dead.

From the hills and valleys earth
Shouts back the sound of mirth,
Tramp of feet and lilt of sing
Ringing all the road along.
All the music of their going,
Ringing swinging glad song-throwing,
Earth will echo still, when foot
Lies numb and voice mute.
  On, marching men, on
  To the gates of death with song.
  Sow your gladness for earth's reaping,
  So you may be glad, though sleeping.
  Strew your gladness on earth's bed,
  So be merry, so be dead.

To Germany

You are blind like us. Your hurt no man designed,
And no man claimed the conquest of your land.
But gropers both through fields of thought confined
We stumble and we do not understand.
You only saw your future bigly planned,
And we, the tapering paths of our own mind,
And in each other's dearest ways we stand,
And hiss and hate. And the blind fight the blind.

When it is peace, then we may view again
With new-won eyes each other's truer form
And wonder. Grown more loving-kind and warm
We'll grasp firm hands and laugh at the old pain,
When it is peace. But until peace, the storm
The darkness and the thunder and the rain.

A Hundred Thousand Million Mites We Go

A hundred thousand million mites we go
Wheeling and tacking o'er the eternal plain,
Some black with death—and some are white with woe.
Who sent us forth? Who takes us home again?

And there is sound of hymns of praise—to whom?
And curses—on whom curses?—snap the air.
And there is hope goes hand in hand with gloom,
And blood and indignation and despair.

And there is murmuring of the multitude
And blindness and great blindness, until some
Step forth and challenge blind Vicissitude
Who tramples on them: so that fewer come.

And nations, ankle-deep in love or hate,
Throw darts or kisses all the unwitting hour
Beside the ominous unseen tide of fate;
And there is emptiness and drink and power.

And some are mounted on swift steeds of thought
And some drag sluggish feet of stable toil.
Yet all, as though they furiously sought,
Twist turn and tussle, close and cling and coil.

A hundred thousand million mites we sway
Writhing and tossing on the eternal plain,
Some black with death—but most are bright with Day!
Who sent us forth? Who brings us home again?

September 1914.

Two Sonnets

I

Saints have adored the lofty soul of you.
Poets have whitened at your high renown.
We stand among the many millions who
Do hourly wait to pass your pathway down.
You, so familiar, once were strange: we tried
To live as of your presence unaware.
But now in every road on every side
We see your straight and steadfast signpost there.

I think it like that signpost in my land,
Hoary and tall, which pointed me to go
Upward, into the hills, on the right hand,
Where the mists swim and the winds shriek and blow,
A homeless land and friendless, but a land
I did not know and that I wished to know.

II

Such, such is Death: no triumph: no defeat:
Only an empty pail, a slate rubbed clean,
A merciful putting away of what has been.

And this we know: Death is not Life effete,
Life crushed, the broken pail. We who have seen
So marvellous things know well the end not yet.

Victor and vanquished are a-one in death:
Coward and brave: friend, foe. Ghosts do not say
"Come, what was your record when you drew breath?"
But a big blot has hid each yesterday
So poor, so manifestly incomplete.
And your bright Promise, withered long and sped,
Is touched, stirs, rises, opens and grows sweet
And blossoms and is you, when you are dead.

June 12, 1915.

[*When You See Millions of the Mouthless Dead*]

When you see millions of the mouthless dead
Across your dreams in pale battalions go,
Say not soft things as other men have said,
That you'll remember. For you need not so.
Give them not praise. For, deaf, how should they know
It is not curses heaped on each gashed head?
Nor tears. Their blind eyes see not your tears flow.
Nor honour. It is easy to be dead.
Say only this, "They are dead." Then add thereto,
"Yet many a better one has died before."
Then, scanning all the o'ercrowded mass, should you
Perceive one face that you loved heretofore,
It is a spook. None wears the face you knew.
Great death has made all his for evermore.

[*There is such change in all those fields*]

There is such change in all those fields,
Such motion rhythmic, ordered, free,
Where ever-glancing summer yields
Birth, fragrance, sunlight, immanency,
To make us view our rights of birth.
What shall we do? How shall we die?
We, captives of a roaming earth,
'Mid shades that life and light deny.

Blank summer's surfeit heaves in mist;
Dumb earth basks dewy-washed; while still
We whom Intelligence has kissed
Do make us shackles of our will.
And yet I know in each loud brain,
Round-clamped with laws and learning so,
Is madness more and lust of strain
Than earth's jerked godlings e'er can know.
The false Delilah of our brain
Has set us round the millstone going.
O lust of roving! lust of pain!
Our hair will not be long in growing.
Like blinded Samson round we go.
We hear the grindstone groan and cry.
Yet we are kings, we know, we know.
What shall we do? How shall we die?
Take but our pauper's gift of birth,
O let us from the grindstone free!
And tread the maddening gladdening earth
In strength close-braced with purity.
The earth is old; we ever new.
Our eyes should see no other sense
Than this, eternally to DO—
Our joy, our task, our recompense;
Up unexploréd mountains move,
Track tireless through great wastes afar,
Nor slumber in the arms of love,
Nor tremble on the brink of war;
Make Beauty and make Rest give place,
Mock Prudence loud—and she is gone,
Smite Satisfaction on the face
And tread the ghost of Ease upon.
Light-lipped and singing press we hard
Over old earth which now is worn,
Triumphant, buffeted and scarred,
By billows howled at, tempest-torn,
Toward blue horizons far away
(Which do not give the rest we need,
But some long strife, more than this play,
Some task that will be stern indeed)—
We ever new, we ever young,
We happy creatures of a day!
What will the gods say, seeing us strung
As nobly and as taut as they?

[I have not brought my Odyssey]

I have not brought my Odyssey
With me here across the sea;
But you'll remember, when I say
How, when they went down Sparta way,
To sandy Sparta, long ere dawn
Horses were harnessed, rations drawn,
Equipment polished sparkling bright,
And breakfasts swallowed (as the white
Of Eastern heavens turned to gold)—
The dogs barked, swift farewells were told.
The sun springs up, the horses neigh,
Crackles the whip thrice—then away!
From sun-go-up to sun-go-down
All day across the sandy down
The gallant horses galloped, till
The wind across the downs more chill
Blew, the sun sank and all the road
Was darkened, that it only showed
Right at the end the town's red light
And twilight glimmering into night.

The horses never slackened till
They reached the doorway and stood still.
Then came the knock, the unlading; then
The honey-sweet converse of men,
The splendid bath, the change of dress,
Then—O the grandeur of their Mess,
The henchmen, the prim stewardess!
And O the breaking of old ground,
The tales, after the port went round!
(The wondrous wiles of old Odysseus,
Old Agamemnon and his misuse
Of his command, and that young chit
Paris—who didn't care a bit
For Helen—only to annoy her
He did it really, κ.τ.λ.)

But soon they led amidst the din
The honey-sweet ἀοιδὸς in,
Whose eyes were blind, whose soul had sight,
Who knew the fame of men in fight—
Bard of white hair and trembling foot,
Who sang whatever God might put
Into his heart.
                        And there he sung,

Those war-worn veterans among,
Tales of great war and strong hearts wrung,
Of clash of arms, of council's brawl,
Of beauty that must early fall,
Of battle hate and battle joy
By the old windy walls of Troy.
They felt that they were unreal then,
Visions and shadow-forms, not men.
But those the Bard did sing and say
(Some were their comrades, some were they)
Took shape and loomed and strengthened more
Greatly than they had guessed of yore.

And now the fight begins again,
The old war-joy, the old war-pain.
Sons of one school across the sea
We have no fear to fight—

*　*　*　*　*

And soon, O soon, I do not doubt it,
With the body or without it,
We shall all come tumbling down
To our old wrinkled red-capped town.
Perhaps the road up Ilsley way,
The old ridge-track, will be my way.
High up among the sheep and sky,
Look down on Wantage, passing by,
And see the smoke from Swindon town;
And then full left at Liddington,
Where the four winds of heaven meet
The earth-blest traveller to greet.
And then my face is toward the south,
There is a singing on my mouth:
Away to rightward I descry
My Barbury ensconced in sky,
Far underneath the Ogbourne twins,
And at my feet the thyme and whins,
The grasses with their little crowns
Of gold, the lovely Aldbourne downs,
And that old signpost (well I knew
That crazy signpost, arms askew,
Old mother of the four grass ways).
And then my mouth is dumb with praise,
For, past the wood and chalkpit tiny,
A glimpse of Marlborough ἐρατεινή!
So I descend beneath the rail
To warmth and welcome and wassail.

* * * * *

This from the battered trenches—rough,
Jingling and tedious enough.
And so I sign myself to you:
One, who some crooked pathways knew
Round Bedwyn: who could scarcely leave
The Downs on a December eve:
Was at his happiest in shorts,
And got—not many good reports!
Small skill of rhyming in his hand—
But you'll forgive—you'll understand.

July 12, 1915.

In Memoriam S.C.W., V.C.

There is no fitter end than this.
    No need is now to yearn nor sigh.
We know the glory that is his,
    A glory that can never die.

Surely we knew it long before,
    Knew all along that he was made
For a swift radiant morning, for
    A sacrificing swift night-shade.

September 8th, 1915.

SELECTED POEMS OF EDGELL RICKWORD

Winter Warfare

Colonel Cold strode up the Line
    (Tabs of rime and spurs of ice);
Stiffened all that met his glare:
    Horses, men and lice.

Visited a forward post,
    Left them burning, ear to foot;
Fingers stuck to biting steel,
    Toes to frozen boot.

Stalked on into No Man's Land,
    Turned the wire to fleecy wool,
Iron stakes to sugar sticks
    Snapping at a pull.

Those who watched with hoary eyes
  Saw two figures gleaming there;
Hauptmann Kälte, colonel old,
  Gaunt in the grey air.

Stiffly, tinkling spurs they moved,
  Glassy-eyed, with glinting heel
Stabbing those who lingered there
  Torn by screaming steel.

Trench Poets

I knew a man, he was my chum,
But he grew blacker every day,
And would not brush the flies away,
Nor blanch however fierce the hum
Of passing shells; I used to read,
To rouse him, random things from Donne—
Like "Get with child a mandrake-root."
But you can tell he was far gone,
For he lay gaping, mackerel-eyed,
And stiff, and senseless as a post
Even when that old poet cried
"I long to talk with some old lover's ghost."

I tried the Elegies one day,
But he, because he heard me say:
"What needst thou have no more covering than a man?"
Grinned nastily, and so I knew
The worms had got his brains at last.
There was one thing that I might do
To starve the worms; I racked my head
For healthy things and quoted "*Maud*."
His grin got worse and I could see
He sneered at passion's purity.
He stank so badly, though we were great chums
I had to leave him; then rats ate his thumbs.

The Soldier Addresses His Body

I shall be mad if you get smashed about;
We've had good times together, you and I;
Although you groused a bit when luck was out,
And women passionless, and we went dry.

Yet there are many things we have not done;
Countries not seen, where people do strange things;
Eat fish alive, and mimic in the sun
The solemn gestures of their stone- grey kings.

I've heard of forests that are dim at noon
Where snakes and creepers wrestle all day long;
Where vivid beasts grow pale with the full moon,
Gibber and cry, and wail a mad old song;

Because at the full moon the Hippogriff,
With crinkled ivory snout and agate feet,
With his green eye will glare them cold and stiff
For the coward Wyvern to come down and eat.

Vodka and kvass, and bitter mountain wines
We have not drunk, nor snatched at bursting grapes
To pelt slim girls among Sicilian vines
Who'd flicker through the leaves, faint frolic shapes .

Yea, there are many things we have not done,
But it's a sweat to knock them into rhyme,
Let's have a drink, and give the cards a run
And leave dull verse to the dull peaceful time.

War and Peace

In sodden trenches I have heard men speak,
Though numb and wretched, wise and witty things;
And loved them for the stubbornness that clings
Longest to laughter when Death's pulleys creak;

And seeing cool nurses move on tireless feet
To do abominable things with grace,
Deemed them sweet sisters in that haunted place
Where, with child's voices, strong men howl or bleat.

Yet now those men lay stubborn courage by,
Riding dull-eyed and silent in the train
To old men's stools; or sell gay-coloured socks
And listen fearfully for Death; so I
Love the low-laughing girls, who now again
Go daintily, in thin and flowery frocks.

SELECTED POEMS BY VARIOUS AUTHORS

For the Fallen

BY LAURENCE BINYON

With proud thanksgiving, a mother for her children,
England mourns for her dead across the sea.
Flesh of her flesh they were, spirit of her spirit,
Fallen in the cause of the free.

Solemn the drums thrill; Death august and royal
Sings sorrow up into immortal spheres,
There is music in the midst of desolation
And a glory that shines upon our tears.

They went with songs to the battle, they were young,
Straight of limb, true of eye, steady and aglow.
They were staunch to the end against odds uncounted;
They fell with their faces to the foe.

They shall grow not old, as we that are left grow old:
Age shall not weary them, nor the years condemn.
At the going down of the sun and in the morning
We will remember them.

They mingle not with their laughing comrades again;
They sit no more at familiar tables of home;
They have no lot in our labour of the day-time;
They sleep beyond England's foam.

But where our desires are and our hopes profound,
Felt as a well-spring that is hidden from sight,
To the innermost heart of their own land they are known
As the stars are known to the Night;

As the stars that shall be bright when we are dust,
Moving in marches upon the heavenly plain;
As the stars that are starry in the time of our darkness,
To the end, to the end, they remain.

In Flanders Fields

BY JOHN MCCRAE

In Flanders fields the poppies blow
Between the crosses, row on row,
      That mark our place; and in the sky
      The larks, still bravely singing, fly
Scarce heard amid the guns below.

We are the Dead. Short days ago
We lived, felt dawn, saw sunset glow,
   Loved and were loved, and now we lie,
            In Flanders fields.

Take up our quarrel with the foe:
To you from failing hands we throw
      The torch; be yours to hold it high.
      If ye break faith with us who die
We shall not sleep, though poppies grow
            In Flanders fields.

The Anxious Dead

BY JOHN MCCRAE

O guns, fall silent till the dead men hear
   Above their heads the legions pressing on:
(These fought their fight in time of bitter fear,
   And died not knowing how the day had gone.)

O flashing muzzles, pause, and let them see
   The coming dawn that streaks the sky afar;
Then let your mighty chorus witness be
   To them, and Caesar, that we still make war.

Tell them, O guns, that we have heard their call,
   That we have sworn, and will not turn aside,
That we will onward till we win or fall,
   That we will keep the faith for which they died.

Bid them be patient, and some day, anon,
   They shall feel earth enwrapt in silence deep;
Shall greet, in wonderment, the quiet dawn,
   And in content may turn them to their sleep.

Festubert, 1916

BY EDMUND BLUNDEN

Tired with dull grief, grown old before my day,
I sit in solitude and only hear
Long silent laughters, murmurings of dismay,
The lost intensities of hope and fear;
In those old marshes yet the rifles lie,
On the thin breastwork flutter the grey rags,
The very books I read are there—and I
Dead as the men I loved, wait while life drags

Its wounded length from those sad streets of war
Into green places here, that were my own;
But now what once was mine is mine no more,
I look for such friends here and I find none.
With such strong gentleness and tireless will
Those ruined houses seared themselves in me,
Passionate I look for their dumb story still,
And the charred stub outspeaks the living tree.

I rise up at the singing of a bird
And scarcely knowing slink along the lane,
I dare not give a soul a look or word
Where all have homes and none's at home in vain:
Deep red the rose burned in the grim redoubt,
The self-sown wheat around was like a flood,
In the hot path the lizard lolled time out,
The saints in broken shrines were bright as blood.

Sweet Mary's shrine between the sycamores!
There we would go, my friend of friends and I,
And snatch long moments from the grudging wars,
Whose dark made light intense to see them by . . .
Shrewd bit the morning fog, the whining shots
Spun from the wrangling wire: then in warm swoon
The sun hushed all but the cool orchard plots,
We crept in the tall grass and slept till noon.

Marching Men

BY MARJORIE PICKTHALL

Under the level winter sky
I saw a thousand Christs go by.
They sang an idle song and free
As they went up to calvary.
News without agenda

Careless of eye and coarse of lip,
They marched in holiest fellowship.
That heaven might heal the world, they gave
Their earth-born dreams to deck the grave.

With souls unpurged and steadfast breath
They supped the sacrament of death.
And for each one, far off, apart,
Seven swords have rent a woman's heart.

My Boy Jack

BY RUDYARD KIPLING

"Have you news of my boy Jack?"
　　Not this tide.
"When d'you think that he'll come back?"
　　Not with this wind blowing, and this tide.

"Has any one else had word of him?"
　　Not this tide.
For what is sunk will hardly swim,
　　Not with this wind blowing, and this tide.

"Oh, dear, what comfort can I find?"
　　None this tide,
　　Nor any tide,
Except he did not shame his kind—
Not even with that wind blowing, and that tide.

Then hold your head up all the more,
　　This tide,
　　And every tide;
Because he was the son you bore,
　　And gave to that wind blowing and that tide!

The Cenotaph

BY CHARLOTTE MEW

Not yet will those measureless fields be green again
Where only yesterday the wild sweet blood of wonderful youth was shed;
There is a grave whose earth must hold too long, too deep a stain,
Though for ever over it we may speak as proudly as we may tread.
But here, where the watchers by lonely hearths from the thrust of an inward
    sword have more slowly bled,
We shall build the Cenotaph: Victory, winged, with Peace, winged too, at
    the column's head.
And over the stairway, at the foot—oh! here, leave desolate, passionate
    hands to spread
Violets, roses, and laurel with the small sweet twinkling country things
Speaking so wistfully of other Springs
From the little gardens of little places where son or sweetheart was born and
    bred.
In splendid sleep, with a thousand brothers
                    To lovers—to mothers
                    Here, too, lies he:
Under the purple, the green, the red,
It is all young life: it must break some women's hearts to see
Such a brave, gay coverlet to such a bed!
Only, when all is done and said,
God is not mocked and neither are the dead.

For this will stand in our Market-place—
                    Who'll sell, who'll buy
                    (Will you or I
Lie each to each with the better grace)?
While looking into every busy whore's and huckster's face
As they drive their bargains, is the Face
Of God: and some young, piteous, murdered face.

This is No Case of Petty Right or Wrong

BY EDWARD THOMAS

This is no case of petty right or wrong
That politicians or philosophers
Can judge. I hate not Germans, nor grow hot
With love of Englishmen, to please newspapers.
Beside my hate for one fat patriot
My hatred of the Kaiser is love true:—
A kind of god he is, banging a gong.
But I have not to choose between the two,

Or between justice and injustice. Dinned
With war and argument I read no more
Than in the storm smoking along the wind
Athwart the wood. Two witches' cauldrons roar.
From one the weather shall rise clear and gay;
Out of the other an England beautiful
And like her mother that died yesterday.
Little I know or care if, being dull,
I shall miss something that historians
Can rake out of the ashes when perchance
The phoenix broods serene above their ken.
But with the best and meanest Englishmen
I am one in crying, God save England, lest
We lose what never slaves and cattle blessed.
The ages made her that made us from dust:
She is all we know and live by, and we trust
She is good and must endure, loving her so:
And as we love ourselves we hate our foe.

The Call

BY JESSIE POPE

Who's for the trench—
    Are you, my laddie?
Who'll follow French—
    Will you, my laddie?
Who's fretting to begin,
Who's going out to win?
And who wants to save his skin—
    Do you, my laddie?

Who's for the khaki suit—
    Are you, my laddie?
Who longs to charge and shoot—
    Do you, my laddie?
Who's keen on getting fit,
Who means to show his grit,
And who'd rather wait a bit—
    Would you, my laddie?

Who'll earn the Empire's thanks—
   Will you, my laddie?
Who'll swell the victor's ranks—
   Will you, my laddie?
When that procession comes,
Banners and rolling drums—
Who'll stand and bite his thumbs—
   Will you, my laddie?

Who's for the Game?

BY JESSIE POPE

Who's for the game, the biggest that's played,
   The red crashing game of a fight?
Who'll grip and tackle the job unafraid?
   And who thinks he'd rather sit tight?

Who'll toe the line for the signal to "Go!"?
   Who'll give his country a hand?
Who wants a turn to himself in the show—
   And who wants a seat in the stand?

Who knows it won't be a picnic—not much—
   Yet eagerly shoulders a gun?
Who would much rather come back with a crutch,
   Than lie low and be out of the fun?

Come along, lads—but you'll come on all right—
   For there's only one course to pursue,
Your country is up to her neck in a fight,
   And she's looking and calling for you.

War Girls

BY JESSIE POPE

There's the girl who clips your ticket for the train,
   And the girl who speeds the lift from floor to floor,
There's the girl who does a milk-round in the rain,
   And the girl who calls for orders at your door.
      Strong, sensible, and fit,
      They're out to show their grit,
   And tackle jobs with energy and knack.
      No longer caged and penned up,
      They're going to keep their end up
Till the khaki soldier boys come marching back.

There's the motor girl who drives a heavy van,
   There's the butcher girl who brings your joint of meat,
There's the girl who cries 'All fares, please!' like a man,
   And the girl who whistles taxis up the street.
          Beneath each uniform
          Beats a heart that's soft and warm,
  Though of canny mother-wit they show no lack;
          But a solemn statement this is,
          They've no time for love and kisses
Till the khaki soldier-boys come marching back.

THE END

www.ingramcontent.com/pod-product-compliance
Lightning Source LLC
Chambersburg PA
CBHW051824040426
42447CB00006B/354